Throwing Rackets and Breaking Records

by Mike Geraghty

Published by Mike Geraghty

Published by Mike Geraghty 2006

ISBN 0-9553685-1-0

9 780955 368516 >

The Author

Mike Geraghty was born in Galway in1962. He graduated from University College Galway in 1983 with a B.Comm Degree and a Higher Diploma in Education in 1984. In 1997 he got a distinction for Sport Psychology in a correspondence course from Kilroy College in Dublin. He has followed Tennis since the late seventies and played competitively since 1982, representing Galway Lawn Tennis Club, University College Galway at Intervarsity level and Connacht at Interprovincial level. When teaching Mike developed Schools Tennis at both Colaiste Iognaid and The Convent of Mercy. In March 2006 Mike was involved in setting up "The Galway Community Tennis Initiative". The idea behind this initiative is to get children and adults playing tennis all year round, and provide an opportunity for everyone to try it out. The highpoint of his career though has been creating with Francis Power a new world record for one pair playing doubles against all-comers of 26 hours competitive tennis in 2003 and re-claiming the world record in 2005 by playing for 36 hours. The two Galway men featured in the 50th anniversary edition of The Guinness Book of Records 2005, 50 years after Roger Bannister broke the record for the first sub four-minute mile. In November 2005 Galway Bay FM honoured Mike and Francis by choosing them as Tennis Sport Stars Of The Year for their achievement. Mike set up the Newcastle Video Library in 1986 and that is where he wrote this book. Mike has also written a fictional book on tennis called Alphabet Tennis.

Dedication

To Michael, Lee and Nicole: Never ever give up!

Introduction

I first got the idea of writing a book when I read an article in the Irish Independent early in September 2003. The article stated that the Irish set more world records per capita than any other country. I thought that this was an incredible statistic, and having set a new world record for a Tennis Doubles Marathon with Francis Power that summer, it was great to be part of that elite group. However my delight at this news was tempered by a nagging doubt that the Guinness Book of World Records was published too early for our inclusion that year.

When Francis and I had set the world record in June, and had it verified in July, we both hoped to feature in that year's edition. I had assumed like most annual publications, that it would be published in December, forgetting obviously that most publications aimed at the Christmas market are released in September. I instinctively knew that we would not make the cut off date, and I phoned my mum Florrie, to check in Eason's if we were in the book. This was very apt, as when I was a kid Florrie used to bring me into Glynn's every autumn, to put aside annuals such as Tiger, Roy of the Rovers and Shoot, so that she could pay them off weekly up to Christmas. No better person to confirm my fear that we had missed the cut off date. On her arrival to Eason's Florrie noticed some kids flicking through the pile of Guinness World Record Books on display. She overheard one schoolboy ask another "Are Mike and Francis in the book?" Unfortunately we weren't and the kids' jaws dropped.

I contained my disappointment on hearing the news, and informed Francis and Marie Gordon, who had administered our record attempt. There was a lot of disappointment around Galway, as people genuinely wanted to claim that they knew someone who was in the Guinness Book of Records! I remember Marion Hanley's disbelief when she heard at reception in the Tennis Club that we were not in it. Marion was our top junior, and played a lot with Francis. I had played her recently as well, and we could both see a great prospect was on her way. I thought to myself that it would be such a boost to all the juniors and anybody interested in tennis, if we were in the next edition. The next day I began campaigning for our inclusion in the following year's book. I wrote a letter to Sophie Whiting, who had been my original contact at GWR, letting her know what a great boost it would be to all the young tennis players in Ireland, and if the criterion to what goes in the book is what a 13 year old would find interesting then I could guarantee that we met this test. A few weeks later I phoned and spoke to another lady, Ann Collins, and she confirmed that the cut off date was May, and that our record still held. In the Spring I contacted Scott Christie, and he again confirmed that we were the official world record holders.

Time passed and the next I heard was when I received a call from Scott, to see would Francis and I be interested in discussing a possible match in Los Angeles, organised by a TV station. Of course we would! Unfortunately due to red tape, nothing came of it. Scott could not give their details to me it was up to them, he insisted to make contact and when I checked back with him he claimed that he had no further details. Very strange, but I assume that they deal with so much information, that errors do occur. However when I asked him to check if our record still stood, he confirmed that it did. Things were looking good, and when I got a call from GWR, to see if I would do an interview with The Examiner in August it suddenly hit me. "Does that mean we are in the Guinness Book of Records?" I enquired of the lady who rang me. When she replied "Yes", I insisted that she double-checked, to be sure to be sure. I was ecstatic. Phone calls to Francis, Marie and anyone I could think of followed, and before I knew it Galway Bay FM wanted us to do a live interview with Keith Finnegan. He knew how big it was and gave us terrific exposure. Oliver Martyn and I did a press release, and by the following week Francis and I featured in all the local press. Not only did we make the Guinness Book Of World Records, but we also realized a dream of mine to be in the 50th Anniversary Edition of The Guinness Book Of Records. Fifty years after Roger Bannister set the first sub four minute mile, two Irishmen set a new World Record for tennis. Beat that!

This book went on the back burner for a while, as we basked in the excitement. Gradually, over the following months, I started to write about our feat. Bit by bit it started to take shape, and when GWR honoured Francis and I, at a 50th Anniversary party in Dublin in November 2004, I discussed my idea of a book on Irish world record holders with some of the GWR team. They were very enthusiastic at the time, and agreed to contact me after Christmas. However, not for the first time, they obviously lost the intention in their workload, and when I contacted Scott in May about getting details of Irish world record holders for research on this book, he informed me that GWR could not give out details of individual record holders, and were not interested in cooperating with promoting one country ahead of others, for holding more world records, as this would cause bad feeling. I'm sure you can imagine my response, and I ended by enquiring if our world record still held. Scott really made my day by informing me that a pair of German players had broken our record! The rest is history…I hope you enjoy it!

Acknowledgements

I would like to acknowledge the following newspapers for their coverage of the two world records. Both in written and photographic form, I would like to mention the following: The Galway Advertiser, The Galway Independent, The Connacht Sentinel, The Connacht Tribune, The City Tribune, Faointe, The Irish Daily Mirror, The Irish Star, The Irish Examiner, The Irish Sunday People, The Irish Times and the Irish Independent. It would be remiss of me not to mention Galway Bay Fm and Red Fm in Cork who covered our success over the air.

Despite numerous phone calls to The Irish Independent offices I was unable to source the original author on the piece about the Irish holding the most world records per capita. I would be only too glad to correct this omission in future editions.I have always been interested in sport psychology and would like to acknowledge the benefit of reading parts of the following books throughout the years : Introduction to Psychology 7th Edition by Ernest Hilgard, Rita L Atkinson and Richard C Atkinson; Sport Psychology: A Self-Help Guide by Stephen J Bull and finally an old tennis playing buddy of mine from a few years back Aidan P Moran who wrote Sport and Exercise Psychology: A Critical Introduction.As it's a motto I very much live by I had better acknowledge Roy Keane's motto "Fail to prepare, Prepare to fail!"

I would like to thank my son Michael for going through the 50th Anniversary Edition of the Guinness Book of World Records in search of Irish World Record Holders. The Guinness Book of World Records was the source of the records held by the caricatures featured on the cover of this book. Following on from her first job of editing Alphabet Tennis, Nollaig Lineen has again tightened up this book; and I continue to be amazed by the thoroughness of her work! Thanks again to Greg Cunningham at Jaycee Quickprint for helping me turn the manuscripts into book form and in particular Graham Cummins, senior graphic designer, who was extremely helpful in producing the final product of 'Alphabet Tennis' and has continued his fine work with 'Throwing Rackets and Breaking Records'. Special thanks to Edwin Brennan, who video taped our second world record in 2005 and scanned the photos and newspaper articles.I would also like to thank Ryno Bruwer who videoed and edited hours of tape for our original record in 2003. Oliver Martyn supplied photographs of both world records, as well as heading up the PR team. Ken Lee has produced a terrific cover and although they say "You can't judge a book by it's cover," I would hope that it will entice many potential readers to pick it up.

Chapter 1

HOW TO SET A WORLD RECORD

Most people set goals in life, some realistic, others less realistic. Note I didn't say impossible because, to set a world record you must believe that nothing is impossible. You need to believe in yourself and to have confidence in those around you. There is no room for self-doubt, and once you choose a course of action you must develop tunnel vision- until you enter the sunlight on the other side. In my case I believe that this confidence in my own ability comes with life experience. In Francis' case I would think it is a combination of youthful enthusiasm, natural cockiness and tremendous determination to succeed. The further I go down the path of life the more I want to leave a legacy of achievement. I do not want to be one of those people who says "I could have….". I'm more interested in saying that I tried, and hopefully, more often than not, succeeded. Too many people drift through life with no purpose, and just are… there has to be more to it than that! At this stage I find that I am more impatient to get things done, and never was there a truer saying than "If you want something done right, do it yourself". When you're a kid the ambitions are generally high: to be a professional footballer; walk on the moon; climb Everest or be a professional tennis player. All of these are attainable with the right blend of hard work, ability, support and luck. The Irish will always add luck, because otherwise life would be very predictable.

In my case I came to tennis late. I had no junior career and only started to play regularly in my early twenties. Until then it was all football. When I finally decided that a career as Player/Manager/Chairman of Leeds United was not on, I started to get into tennis. Football was getting harder to organise, as you relied on large numbers, and there was no real commitment to regular games. I had decided that I intended to stay fit throughout my life, and wanted a sport that I could play regularly and all year round. Over the years different people recommended tennis, noting that I was a good athlete and an individual sport would probably suit me. From time to time I would catch the odd match on TV, being particularly drawn to any Jimmy Connors game, particularly if it involved Bjorn Borg or John McEnroe. Jimmy brought the street fighter element to what I had perceived as an upper-class type sport, and once he and Mac got together the fireworks would start. I loved watching Connors and Borg battle it out, the Street fighter versus the Iceman. That's what sport is all about: balance and competition. Ice and Fire. 1982, eight years after winning his first Wimbledon title, Connors defeated McEnroe in a classic 5 set encounter. Borg had quit, and the minute I heard he wasn't playing Wimbledon, I knew Connors would win.

University College Galway, where I was studying commerce, had no structure to its tennis club, so I joined Galway Lawn Tennis Club. My first tournament was an American Tournament, a round robin mixed doubles and my partner Mary Bourke and I finished runners-up. I still maintain that we would have won, if my soon- to- be friend Barry O' Donovan hadn't clocked Mary with a smash early on in the final, and after that he and Helen Kelly went on to win 6-3. Frank Hayden was the tennis captain at the time, and it was his encouragement and enthusiasm that developed my interest in getting further involved at GLTC. Shortly after, I was selected for the inaugural Winter league sub-committee, and we developed all year round tennis for the first time in Galway. I've been fortunate enough to win many tournaments since that summer of 1982, play Inter-Varsity for UCG, Veteran Inter-Provincial for Connacht and captain GLTC to victories in Day Cups, Galway Leagues, Connacht Junior Cups, Inter-County Cups and win events at all the Tournaments that we have hosted in Galway throughout the years.

Surprisingly for someone perceived as suited to an individual sport, my main success has been in doubles. However I have won singles events at The Whit Weekend City of Galway Championship, The Club Championship and The October Weekend Connacht Open and been ranked as high as No. 3 on the club ladder. I derive more satisfaction from doubles though, and the three events I enjoyed most were winning the Mixed Doubles in Club Week 1990 with Clodagh Hobbs, the 1998 City of Galway Championships Doubles with Justin Glynn, and the 2002 Turkey Tournament with John Fennelly. The most satisfying team wins I participated in were both at provincial level. In 1991 GLTC travelled to Castlebar to try and reclaim the Connacht Cup. Sligo, who held it for the previous two years, were extremely cocky, and I remember their captain wondering if they should bother taking the cup out of the car boot, as it would be returning to Sligo. Big mistake! A short motivational speech from their captain and the Galway team of Gerry Riordan, Donncha Harkin, Ruth Glynn, Margaret Murphy and Josie Kelly (R.I.P.) kicked ass. The cup returned to Galway. A similarly smug Sligo team were again sent home empty handed in 1999, when needing to win by 14 points in the last match the Moore sisters produced a 16-1 victory. I will never forget this match. I did not tell them how much they needed to win by and watched the match from behind a curtain in the clubhouse. I knew if I was out courtside willing them on they might have become nervous. Great leadership!

The bi-yearly team events at GLTC are also great for team spirit, and Donal Hegarty and myself are always fighting it out to see who has won the most. I claim the best run, leading teams to victories in three consecutive team events between 1999 and 2000. So you can see that although I am very single-minded I do get tremendous satisfaction in contriving team victories. I believe that there are far more variables in the doubles game, and I enjoy when the overall effort of a group of individuals is combined to produce a team victory. I think in hindsight that the more people who share the victory, the more satisfying it is. That's why it was such a terrific feeling when people claimed that they were part of a world record, having either helped organise, play or supported us in achieving it.

The question that I am asked most about our world record attempts is "What training did you do to prepare yourself to play Tennis for so long"? Well, as Francis and I both said in 2003, we both played a few times a week, and we came into the event without any major injuries. I know that second time round Francis is playing and coaching most days, as well as doing a bit of gym work. It has helped him, and his game continues to improve, as he gets fitter, faster and stronger. In my case its more natural conditioning, as I play twice a week, upping this level during tournaments (which unfortunately are few and far between). I walk my dog, Spike, a Border Collie, every day, irrespective of the weather. Having played sport all my life, not drinking or smoking and keeping active, I feel I can maintain a good fitness level. Also, you get to know what your body is capable of enduring, and even though I do have a persistent elbow problem and the odd niggling injury, I do not feel it detracts much from my performance.

I like to think that while maintaining my physical fitness I am strong mentally as well. I would consider myself generally very positive, and having served on committees and boards over the years, I was well up to the inevitable political challenge when it arose. I find myself more attuned with current affairs than before I entered the political arena, and do believe I can make a difference. One thing I find is that if people do not pull their own weight, and show similar commitment to a cause, I will add up the pros and cons before committing my time and efforts to it. I also find that I am very impatient to get things done, though I don't see this as a negative. So the idea was that Francis and I would approach each record attempt in the best health and condition possible, without making any drastic changes to our routines in the weeks leading up to the marathon. If you come into the task clean, then you have a better chance of surviving the inevitable cramp and strains that you will pick up in any endurance event. Francis and I, being individuals, would worry about getting ourselves prepared for the event, knowing fully that the other would do what suited them. It worked first time round, so why change a winning strategy. From my point of view I felt that if we had more physio, had plenty of fuel, whether it was pasta or pitta, and felt comfortable with what we were doing we would be fine. Once on court we didn't want any distractions. That meant we didn't need to worry about players, stewards, or even public officials not turning up! Only joking Brian, I enjoy a challenge. It keeps me focussed. A month before the marathon I had played six matches in two days with no reaction or loss of condition, so I knew I was ready.

The key to the mental side is to be relaxed, having prepared well beforehand, gone through the various difficulties, thought about what you would do given certain situations, and then to just focus on each match one at a time. The physical side was more likely to cause problems as you can never legislate against injuries, just plan for the best possible treatment if they happen, and I was happy enough that thanks to Erin Ryan, Ger Brennan and Rita Halloran that was in hand. People wondered how we were both able to hit tennis balls, and relatively well I'm told, for 36 hours. You develop a rhythm after hitting so many and I can honestly say that in neither marathon did I get as much as a twinge from my elbow. Most injuries occur when players are not sufficiently warmed up- this was not a problem for us. Certainly eating more, and at regular intervals, helped me, although I never felt that tired on either occasion. In both marathons Francis picked up shoulder injuries. In 2003 I got some cramp in my left thigh and knee and in 2005 my left calf got a bit tight. I must discuss this with the physios, to see how I can eliminate this in future. But the fact that we were both back playing in the Inter-Counties Cup the following weekend, says a lot for our conditioning and fitness level. The toughest thing I found was not playing tennis for a week!

So with all this knowledge if you still want to set a world record, you need to follow these steps:
1.Decide what record you want to set.
2.Contact Guinness World Records by phone or on-line.
3.Put together a good back up team.
4. Pick a date. When you get your claim number from GWR, register it.
5.Plan the event thoroughly. Leave no stone unturned.
6. Prepare yourself mentally and physically for the task ahead.
7. Do it. Then meticulously put the proof together for verification.
8. Check directly to ensure GWR received information, and wait patiently until you receive your certificate from The Keeper Of The Records.
9. Good luck!

Chapter 2

THE DAY WE SET A NEW WORLD RECORD

The idea of setting a world record first came to me, in the spring of 2002. I was reading about a forthcoming attempt at a tennis marathon, in a tennis magazine. I remember thinking that I would be interested in organising such an event. However the timing wasn't right. I was approaching the end of my fourth tennis captaincy at Galway Lawn Tennis Club, the coaching team were breaking up, and I knew that would take a lot of time to sort out during the summer and, most importantly, a new baby was due in the Geraghty household in August.

It was during a conversation with the club president, Pat Folan, that the idea came back to my mind. She was asking me about new ideas for fundraising, and I mentioned a marathon. Pat developed the idea of keeping a court going throughout the night, with different combinations playing doubles, and a contribution made to Rehab. In August 2002 I contacted the Guinness World Records in London, and checked to see was there a world record for a tennis marathon. I visualized getting a large group together, and playing for 48 hours from 7pm on a Friday evening through to 7pm on the Sunday evening. However the GWR researchers informed me, that they would only recognise it, as a world record if it was the same players throughout or at least one pair taking on all-comers.

I immediately asked the GWR researcher Sophie Whiting to send me on all the relevant information /conditions/stipulations for a world record attempt, with the intention of attempting it in late August/early September 2002. However, the information did not arrive in time, and I postponed the plans until the summer of 2003. I wanted to attempt the record at the optimum time, with the best possible conditions i.e. weather, temperature, light and interest in tennis. I chose mid-summer, as this should, theoretically, give me the best light, and the temperature should be just right-not too warm and not too cold. Also, our worse adversary in Galway-rain should be less likely. You have to be extremely optimistic and positive to believe that you can set a world record. If you believe, then anything is possible.

I announced my plan at a board meeting in February and was greeted with optimism and enthusiasm. I set up a small sub-committee, to organise the event. Gai Barry, the club Public Relations Officer, ably assisted by tennis P.R.O. Oliver Martyn, headed up the PR team. Marie Gordon, the club administrator, became event administrator. She was certainly the glue that bound everything together. Nicky Nash sourced food, the clock for the event and, as always in charity events that I have been involved in, donations. Nicky and I had previously been involved in organising a men's and ladie's doubles event, raising 480 euro the previous summer, and would be involved in co-coordinating a Special Olympics fun day, raising over 1600 euro in May 2003. The target for our GWR attempt would be to raise 1000 euro for the Galway branch of the Mentally Handicapped. Sinead Barry, who has been invaluable over the years at open tennis events in Galway, personally took responsibility for the logbook to verify our record attempt. This was vital-if this was not 100% accurate the attempt would fail!!! But I had total confidence in her ability, from working with her in the past. Matt O' Connor, the Sports Officer, at GLTC, provided constant enthusiasm, and kept reminding us that we were making history. Grainne Coll contributed by finding a physio who would be on call to us throughout the night, and supported us with ideas and encouragement throughout.

The obvious question here is how did I select my partner for the event? Well I thought of my regular doubles partner John Fennelly, first. In fairness to John, the resilient Corkman was willing to give it a go but he had been out for 5 months with an injury and was rehabilitating gradually. He told me to consider other options. I was driving out to the club for our regular Thursday doubles match with Francis Power and I mentioned my conversation with John. Immediately he said that he wanted to do it! Problem solved. To quote John Lennon: "there are no problems only solutions". So the game was afoot!!!

"Fail to prepare. Prepare to fail!" So said Roy Keane, and how true these words are. Nothing was going to be left to chance in this world record attempt. I didn't want to overburden Francis with thoughts of success or failure, so we did not discuss the marathon too much in the preceding weeks. We were playing tennis on Tuesday and Thursday nights and I knew that he was playing, on average, 5 days a week. No more than the aforementioned Roy Keane, I know just what pace to set my body, having experienced persistent elbow injuries for the last ten years, and a few old injuries from football. I was conscious that to be at my mental and physical peak for the marathon, I wanted to be clear of injuries and well rested. Of course, I thought of it a lot, but I was supremely confident that we would succeed. I suggested some running for stamina purposes, as I had done a lot of this when I played for University College Galway, but Francis wasn't too keen. So I went for a run myself one night, after my usual two-hour doubles stint. I felt fine, but realised that whereas my tennis fitness and endurance levels were A1, I would probably have to do more running if I were to play football on a regular basis. Like any sport you use different muscles, and pressurise different parts of your body, depending on what you are doing. At that point I felt that Francis and I were both in good enough shape to compete for 26 hours.

Why 26 hours? Well a marathon is 26 miles (to the nearest mile), and we did discuss doing more once we reached our stated target but to quote my partner "I'm walking off the court after 26 hours!" That pretty much decided it. In hindsight we could have done more. But it's extremely satisfying to set a target, and attain it, with more gas in the engine. Any of the greats will always maintain that it's nice to get out while you're still ahead. Of course people were sceptical, as the time got closer. My wife, Michelle, felt that we would struggle to get through the night without sleep. A lot of people wondered how we would cope with hitting "the wall". There were those, who asked: "What happens if one of you gets injured?" That brings me onto the medical side of the event.

There are fairly stringent conditions to conforming to the requirements to achieve a world record and have it recognised. Lets be honest, if it was easy any idiot could do it, and given some particular entries in the GWR book, some have. You need to have everything documented: a logbook to record participants, stewards, spectators, doctors, physios, administrators, independent witnesses, injury time-outs, breaks conforming to exact times as in professional sport, videos, pictures, clocks, press cuttings, radio interviews etc. So you can see, that the sub committee that worked with Francis and myself were very busy, and dedicated people.

I wrote to doctors and physios, and rang independent witnesses, while the rest of the group worked on food, stewards, and press etc. There was a very positive response, and I believe people were a little excited to participate in something that, for me, was to become the single biggest event in the history of Galway Lawn Tennis Club, and certainly all those who participated in it. As I mentioned earlier, everything had to be spot on. Even more so, as GWR cannot physically send people out to monitor every single world record attempt! In fact the summer of 2003 produced many world records in Ireland alone. Richard Donovan recorded 3 world records on a threadmill in a 48 hour period; a man went up and down Croagh Patrick 7 times in one day; another man set a record for shaking hands, at a fair; and there was a record for the number of people participating in a table quiz, also set in

Galway. There must have been something in the air!

The week leading up to the marathon was very exciting. The highpoint for me was when the headline "Tennis 2 to Net Record" appeared in Tuesday's Daily Mirror. To appear in a paper that you have read since your schooldays is quite a kick, I can tell you. (Due to time constraints, I only read the Irish Independent now!) A friend of mine, Donal Hegarty, had said to me that Oliver Martyn, the tennis P.R.O., had been in contact with the Daily Mirror, re the forthcoming event. In anticipation I quickly ran through the sports section. Where else would you find something about tennis? To no avail. I was sitting out in the sun (naturally topping up the tan for the marathon) in my back yard, speed-reading through the rest of the paper, as you do, when on the same page as an article on Westlife, I spotted the headline. Within minutes I had a phone call from John Mangan, the Chairman of the Board at GLTC, "Mike, you're in the Daily Mirror, this is big!" And it was! There followed a snippet in extra-time, in the Galway Independent on Wednesday, an article in the Galway Advertiser, and a picture, with a caption, regarding the forthcoming marathon/world record attempt in the Connacht Tribune on Thursday as well. Now the pressure was on...we had to succeed. I, personally, could never live it down if we didn't. Francis was getting into the swing of it, and realising how big this could be. On the Wednesday morning, the two of us did a live radio interview with Olly Turner and Jimmy Norman on Galway Bay FM. These guys were brilliant. Gai Barry, the club P.R.O., had sent out press releases to the papers, and set up the interview. Gai and Oliver Martyn kept the publicity levels very high in the lead up to the event, during it, and in the aftermath. So the buzz was incredible.

I have done a few interviews over the years with GBFM, to promote tennis, for open events and to promote the club for open days. But this was the most fun I've had. Jimmy Norman had attempted a world record, attempting to DJ for 72 hours, prior to our interview, so he knew exactly what we were about, and what sort of commitment was involved. Olly Turner was the main sports reporter, and both showed terrific enthusiasm, for what we were attempting. It was great to see tennis getting such a platform in a city dominated by Gaelic games, with the other main interest coming from football, with Galway United. We explained our plan- to play 14 pairs over a 26 hour period- encouraged the public to come out and see us (a GWR attempt has to be open at all times to the public), and very importantly, put out a call for help, from physios. To be impartial, we put up a board for players to fill in their names, to play us, throughout the 26-hour period. This meant we would have a great variety in ability levels, and everybody from juniors to veterans, from social players to hardened tournament competitors, could participate. Marie Gordon, the club administrator, had overseen this, and more importantly, ensured we had sufficient stewards, doctors and physios to cover the entire 26 hours. Nothing could be left to chance. The lads on the radio announced they were sure that by 4pm on the Saturday we would be world record holders. May the force be with us!

Friday June 21st 2003 was a bright sunny day. I walked the dog, called into my video library, phoned the film reps at National Cable Vision and Columbia Tri-Star, and confirmed that their companies were both going to give a donation of 160 euro each to charity, for my participation in the marathon. Michelle drove Francis and myself to the club, and my two youngest children, Lee and Nicole, came with us. Sorcha Barry videoed our entrance to the tennis club, and we met two of the independent witnesses, who had to monitor our record attempt.

Brendan Kelly is a man I've known for nearly 30 years. He taught me Geography in "The Jes", and was actively involved in cross-country in the school. When I returned to do my teaching practice for the Higher Diploma in Education, Brendan was my tutor. We became good friends, and I started a tennis club in the school. Brendan took a great interest in this, and as well as playing against the pupils in practice, he would drive the teams to matches if I had lectures. In fact, when I had moved on to teach in the Convent of Mercy, where I also set up a tennis club, Brendan would combine the driving for both teams when we travelled to Castlebar etc. Frank Hayden did more than anyone, to get me involved in tennis. He was Tennis Captain at GLTC, when I started playing competitively in 1982. He must have spotted something, as he invited me to serve on the inaugural Winter tennis sub-committee that autumn, which was when Winter tennis got well and truly kick-started in Galway. Iggy O' Muircheartaigh, who is currently president of NUIG, was another member of this committee, and he was lecturing me in Statistics, during my B.Comm. degree, at the time. I wonder did it give me an edge! Only joking, Iggy. I then went on to serve on the senior tennis committee, with Frank that Spring and the two of us virtually ran it for the next three years. Frank moved on from the club around the mid to late eighties, but I went on to become tennis secretary, and then tennis captain on four occasions. So you can see why I chose these two gentlemen. I could rely on them totally. The third independent witness, Michael Needham, was a friend of Frank's, and I believe he was out to see us on more occasions than anyone else, during the 26-hour period. A truly independent witness, with no connections to Francis or myself, who immersed himself totally in the task of verifying a world record.

Gai had invited the Mayor, Val Hanley, to open the proceedings, and we were delighted when his office indicated that he would come. One memory I will always treasure is of the moment we were preparing for the official photograph. As Francis and I stood either side of the mayor, my youngest son Lee, took to the umpire's chair, and my daughter Nicole proceeded to lower the net. She obviously wanted to give Dad every advantage, during the marathon. 2 pm sharp I served the opening ball, in our world record attempt. Unfortunately it wasn't an ace, but it started a lively encounter with Tommy Hehir and Leah Smith. I had actually introduced Tommy to tennis, and much to my regret, was soundly dumped out of the club championships by him, in my first round defence of the title I had won the previous Summer. This, only a few short years after I had taught the badminton champion how to master the outdoor sport. Tommy holds the record for the fastest serve in the West of Ireland, at 119 miles per hour. Leah was ranked in the top 10 juniors in Ireland under-10, and is developing into quite a player. Boy, can she rally crosscourt! We beat them in three sets and declined our 5-minute hourly breaks at 3 and 4 o clock so we could accumulate time for physio treatment, which I knew we would require throughout the marathon.

Next up were Oliver Martyn and Mairtin O' Morain. Again, we soaked up the Mid-Summer sunshine, and swept to a straight sets victory. We should probably have used more sunscreen, and both took a fair bit of sun. We were drinking a lot of fluid throughout the event, but could not overly digest anything heavy. Michelle brought us sausage rolls and chicken, but all I could manage was a couple of bites. Francis was much the same. It took me nearly four hours to get through a ham sandwich. Thanks to Marie we had chocolate and Nicky had got us plenty of bananas and oranges, from Ernie and Eamonn Deacy. Dr Ger Brennan, the first doctor to reply to my request, who actually suggested that we might need more psychological treatment than medical attention, told us we had to eat more, to keep up our energy levels. Francis was drinking lucozade sport and water alternately, but I could only take water I found the lucozade sport too heavy. So Gerry came up with a mix of 7-up and water, for me. This was a great help, as I got energy from the sugar, but it was also diluted with the water, and easy to digest.

At this stage the crowd was beginning to build up and it was great to see so many enthusiastic faces there. I know a lot of people wondered could we last the 26 hours. We never doubted it but I was later told that Paddy Power bookies were taking bets at 3 to 1 against us doing it. If I had known I would have organised a big wager! This was a momentous period, because apart from our marathon, Nelson Mandela was addressing NUIG on the Friday, and the Special Olympics were starting in Dublin on the Saturday. As well as that, the club championships were at the semi-final stage. The one disappointment for me, was that having justified our 4th seeding in the doubles,

John Fennelly and I were due to play Donal Hegarty and Gerry Mannion in the semi-final. I had requested that the match be put back to the Sunday morning, with the final in the afternoon, as Gerry had been away, and unable to play prior to the Saturday. But the committee withdrew me from the tournament, obviously believing that I would not be fit to play after the marathon. In hindsight had I been given the option of playing straight after the marathon or be defaulted, I would certainly have played. All through my life, people say to me "You can't have everything" I say "Why not"? Had I teamed up with Francis for the club championships, then we could have incorporated it into the marathon. Food for thought?

Next up were John Mangan and Angela Dowling. Another entertaining match, where for the only time in the event, Francis and I had words. Francis hit a few double faults, and I said something like "I don't need this for 26 hours" and Francis retorted with "You must be joking if you think I am going to play serious tennis for 26 hours!" Anyone listening must have questioned whether we would be able to last another 22 hours. Interestingly enough, within four hours of starting everybody we talked to was telling us to take it easy and conserve our energy. But that's not the way we play. It's all or nothing!

Nicky Nash and Tim Jones were our 8 o clock opponents. The England/Wales combination were well up for this match and Tim, in particular, held nothing back. I had never seen the "dragon" hit as many winners at the net, or get so many first serves in, since we teamed up in the Winter team tennis event last November. Nicky picked up an injury, and we clawed our way back to victory in the third set. This was followed by a genuine rivalry with John Fennelly and Brian McGoldrick. Before this match, we took a twenty minute accumulated break. Francis got treatment on his neck and I had a rubdown for cramp. As I often get after playing a lot of soccer, I had a fair bit of tightening in my right quad, but I always respond well to physio and Aofainne Walshe had me back to full fitness in ten minutes. Speaking of physios, I cannot stress how vital they were in our pursuit of the record. Sharon Morris came out to check on us at 6pm, and felt we should be fine until Aofainne came at 10 pm. We had agreed only to take injury time-outs if necessary, and to save as much of our hourly five minutes rest time for treatment, as we could. Also, we were better off to keep going and not get cold as the evening went on. The 90-second breaks we got after the third and then every two games in a set, barely allowed a swig of a drink and a square of chocolate, or bite of a banana.

During our break at 10 pm Donal Dempsey told me that we were overdoing it, and to take it easier, as we had to pace ourselves better to complete the marathon. I have known Donal, since I started playing in the club in 1982. He has been a great inspiration to me and many other people he has met over the years, as a player, administrator, and someone with a genuine love of tennis and sport in general. He is the role model for us all, as he plays more often in his early eighties, than most of us manage in an average week. Donal is proof positive that tennis is indeed a sport for life. However, as much respect as I have for him, I was not able to put his advice into practice, especially as John Fennelly started like a dervish, in our next match, trying to blow Francis and myself off the court. Good man John, you never ever give less than 100%. This was a good competitive match, and despite us having had the upper hand in our last few Thursday night duels, the lads beat us by 2 sets to 1. People had been saying: " If you win all your matches you will not get the record". "GWR will say it was fixed". I would have been prepared to argue the case with them if it came to it, but the lads solved that problem. Brian had been very helpful with advice on diet and what medication to take. His advice, which we strictly adhered to, was this: "Take nothing that you wouldn't normally use when playing and don't eat anything that might upset your system". " Also, and most importantly, drink an awful lot of water in the days leading up to the marathon." You know the old saying about hydration in sport: "if you're thirsty,it`s too late". Surprisingly, since their victory that night, we have found it much harder to beat this pair on a Thursday night. No doubt we will correct this. (Postscript: we did!)

As midnight struck, it was the ladies turn to test us after 10 hours on court. Grainne Coll and Sinead Barry provided some light entertainment for the crowd, and us as we had a laugh and eased off a little. I even gave the right arm a rest, and played a few shots with my left, but not getting enough serves in soon put an end to that. The crowd began to play their part at this stage with music, dancing and even an attempt at a Mexican wave, as well as Tommy Hehir, who was now becoming M.C. for the event. Tommy had provided some interesting umpiring earlier. During the match with Oliver Martyn and Mairtin O' Morain, the banter sometimes threatened to turn to violence, with Tommy's commentary on Mairtin`s serving. The crowd, who starting taking up ballboy/ballgirl duty, were very important to us as the night went on. Their shouting and encouragement kept our spirits up. Colette Murphy deserves special mention as, after a long night stint, she returned to see us through the final matches on Saturday. Dr Stephen Higgins, as well as providing medical cover, umpired the midnight match.

The 2am match was one we were looking forward to, as were the crowd. The Sports Administrator Matthew O' Connor, and Club Treasurer Micheal O' Morain, were keen to pit their wits and talents against the marathon men. Matt was one of the few people who, from day one, had ultimate confidence that we would achieve our goal. Very popular with the members and full of enthusiasm, Matt and Micheal were well up for this. Micheal had been organising a bar-b-q for the event and keeping the bar going, so he was probably delighted for a break and an opportunity to play tennis. The lads took the first set, and we had to dig deep to level it off at a set all. If they were up for it, the next match would really test us to the limits.

Neil McLoughlin only plays to win, and if he can break your spirit on the way he will do it. That's why I made him a regular on our Tuesday night, eight man doubles. Whereas his mum, Margaret, one of the best Connacht players ever, tried to give us a chance, Neil would rally us from side to side, and tried, at least twice, to take the head off his great friend and rival, Francis. No danger of dozing off after 15 or 16 hours on court! We took the first set, they levelled it, and then handed us our second defeat in eight matches. One of the main features of the match was the banter between Tommy Hehir (it seemed like he was there all the time) and Neil. It's a pity Tommy, who in fairness antagonised "killer" with his commentary, didn't default him, as it would have made life a lot easier on Francis and myself.

During the 2am match Marie made toast and tea, but we hardly had time to have it. I remember at one stage looking over to the crowd and seeing the security guys who patrol the club at night, having tea and taking it all in. Marie was excellent throughout. She maintains she went home for a Chinese take-away and watched Eastenders, but I think she dreamt this, as I can't ever remember her not being there. Nobody put as much effort (apart from the two guys on court) into ensuring the success of this operation. Sinead Barry, who compiled the logbook, and also seemed omnipresent, was another vital component of our team. Sinead has so much experience of helping with open tennis events, marathons, Special Olympic fundraisers etc; I could see her walk on to the organising committee for the championships at Wimbledon. Sometime during this match we had police intervention. A local Garda, on his way home from work, came in to object to the noise levels. I assume it was the music, which kept up the dwindling crowd's spirits throughout the early hours, and not the arguing between killer and the umpire. Obviously being engrossed in the match, none of the players were aware of the problem until the next changeover, but the umpire made some comment about a stripper, which I'm glad our local Garda didn't hear. It would have been a shame to have our record attempt thwarted, due to being in the Salthill Garda cells.

As we were truly into a bright new day, the dawn shift brought us Gai Barry and Terry Powell. In every marathon the experts claim you hit " the wall". Whereas Francis and I both maintain that we did not hit the wall, in hindsight, this was the most difficult period for us. We were obviously both tired and coming down from a couple of tight matches. Mentally we needed to ease off and physically we were both feeling the toll of over sixteen hours on court. I was experiencing a pain behind my left knee, and felt that I may have to hobble through the next ten hours. Francis also felt tired and had taken quite a bit of sun on the Friday. I called for a physio and Marie contacted the unfortunate Claire Cullinane, who was out by 6.35am. I was aware that I needed treatment, so I asked her could she wait until 7 am, as I would have aggregated some rest time, along with my 3 minutes injury treatment time. Once Claire said it was only cramp, I got a new lease of life and never looked back. She massaged my legs and got the knots out of the knee area. We played probably our worst match quality-wise against Gai and Terry who, in fairness to them, took it fairly easy on us, and we were heading for a set-all draw, when time was up.

The next match was just the tonic we needed. It was a nice easy knockabout with two lovely ladies, Denise Dunne and Emer O' Beirne. Denise had turned up to see us play on Friday, and I assumed she was one of the physios. It was quite funny, because we were discussing conditioning etc until I figured out that she was playing us in the morning. Francis got treatment on his shoulder at 9 am from Caroline Reynolds, and no wonder, he played far better afterwards. I went to Caroline for treatment on my perennial elbow injury a few months later, and touch wood, with her preventative treatment, I feel better than I have for ages. At this stage, we were convinced we would get through to 4 pm. Marie again came to the rescue. Whereas Francis was up for a large breakfast roll, all I could digest was rice crispies. But off she went at 8 am to source food for us.

It was only fitting that Marie and Sarah Caulfield who had returned in the early hours of Saturday morning from a Bon Jovi concert in Dublin, to support us should be our next match. This was the match we had the most fun in. Considering that neither lady played competitive tennis as such, we had some amazing rallies at the net and the crowd got into it. The girls reckon they took it easy on us, as they knew that after eighteen hours we must be tired. Mentally we were now very strong, and funny enough when you hit so many tennis balls, you really get into a groove and there is no effort in hitting groundstrokes and serves. Just as well, for the next match produced the best tennis of the entire event.

If you were to recollect one match from the event this was it! There was a great rivalry between Francis Power and Francis O' Connell and, no more than our old buddy Neil McLoughlin both hate to lose. I wonder why I enjoy playing and competing with these guys so much? Ronan Neacy was Francis` partner, and all I can say about Ronan is that he is just as tough a competitor as his dad Tom. Thank God he wasn't playing, as he would have rallied us to death. The first set went to a tiebreak. The crowd were amazed, as the quality of tennis improved, the closer the match went. None of us were holding back, and we all had our own reasons to win. As we neared 2.24 pm which was the official world record time of 24 hours 24 minutes the crowd began to flow in. Ralph O' Gorman had arrived from Galway Bay Fm, and he was speaking with Margaret McLoughlin. We could hear his commentary, and this was drawing in many of the older members, along with non-members who wanted to be part of something historical. Francis and Ronan went 6-1 up in the tiebreak, and in one of the greatest comebacks ever seen at GLTC; we came back and won 8-6. This gave us such a buzz. Now we were setting a new world record and in style! I could hear Ralph speaking in amazement, about how hard we were hitting the ball and chasing down every shot after a full day on court. We were on a total high. The match ended in a set all draw, and the excitement was such that at one stage umpire Tony Murphy forgot the score. But I knew it!

At 2 pm the President of GLTC Patricia Folan and Dabnet Heery came on court. Every stroke was being applauded at this stage, and everyone wanted to be a part of it. At 2.25 pm the club nearly exploded with cheering, as we shattered the world record. Francis and I exchanged a quick grin and continued on with the task at hand. To finish off, Olwyn Raftery, former President of GLTC and Tennis Ireland, replaced Dabnet, and she was well motivated for the occasion . There were some great rallies, with the two ladies playing full out to stretch us. At 4 pm we had achieved our goal of 26 hours on court; the tennis marathon was completed! The crowd counted down from ten and the rafters shook as GLTC celebrated. I remember throwing my racket in the air, and Francis and I shook hands. Mission accomplished. To achieve something you plan so thoroughly, and invest so much time in, is extremely satisfying. As the champagne flowed, we shook so many hands and saw so many happy and proud faces, Frank Sullivan, a long time club member whose family I would have played a lot of tennis with in my early years at GLTC, even came from a wedding to be there. I can still picture him in the monkey suit, with a huge grin on his face. All the flags were on display. I remember demanding at one stage that we have the Irish Tricolour - if a few guys going up a mountain can have it, then we should do.

As we were interviewed live on air by Ralph O' Gorman for Galway Bay Fm, I proudly saw a mass of flags above us, the Irish flag, the GLTC flag, Galway flag and even the Salthill G.A.A. flag. My eldest son, Michael, and my daughter, Nicole, stood alongside us for the official picture, along with Brendan Kelly, Frank Hayden, Donal Dempsey (whom I had to cajole into being in the picture), Margaret McLoughlin, Olwyn Raftery and many more. Lee had more important things to do, helping his granny build a shed. Kids have a knack of putting everything in perspective. But he did meet the Mayor. I will never forget Ralph O' Gorman's commentary, as we set the record on court 7 at 2.25 pm on Saturday June 21st 2003: " On the weekend that Nelson Mandela came to Galway, and the Special Olympics are starting in Dublin, two Galway men are setting a new world record in tennis."

The next day, just to show that we were fully recovered and still had plenty of gas in the tank, even on the Saturday, Francis and I arrived separately, to watch the singles finals of Club week. It was probably something psychologically we both felt was necessary. To return to the scene of the great event. That night all the competitors attended the Club Championships presentation, at Camelot. Stan Mortimer, the new club champion, made a great speech, culminating in a standing ovation for our great feat. It was like winning an Oscar, to see all those people standing up clapping for us. In the days that followed, we got great acclaim. Our World Record was acknowledged in the Irish Examiner, the Daily Star, and the Galway Independent printed photos of us with the Mayor prior to the marathon, and with the club flag and crowd (including Michael and Nicole) at the end. I did interviews with 'Faointe' (an Irish magazine), the Galway Advertiser and the Connacht Tribune. Francis was inundated with well-wishers at Camelot (where he worked), and shortly after doing an interview with the Connacht Tribune, I believe, the enormity of the event began to hit him.

We were voted Galway Bay Fm Sports Stars of the week, and followed that with another interview with Jimmy and Olly. It gave us an opportunity to thank all the sponsors, and all who contributed to the success of the event. Money-wise we had raised over 800 euro, but as the target of 1000 had not been reached I was determined to reach my goal. So we had the "Fastest Serve in the West Competition" on Sunday 29th June. This was a really fun afternoon, and those who attended, including a father and son from Ballinasloe who heard us on the radio, had a great time, with strawberries and cream, service record attempts and exhibition matches. Marie again was overall co-coordinator, and ensured the event ran smoothly. Paul Noone, on the verge of turning pro at squash, hit the fastest serve on the day of 104 miles per hour. However Tommy Hehir still holds the record, for fastest serve in

14

GLTC at 119 miles per hour, registered in our club Open Day in November 2002.

Having beaten the previous record of 24 hours 24 minutes, we now had to have our record attempt verified. This involved Marie, Gai, Francis, Oliver and myself getting together, with all the press clippings, photographs, log-books,doctor`s certificates, letters from independent witnesses etc. I can't stress enough the importance of some-one like Marie as administrator of the event co-coordinating all the info, double checking, at my insistence, every-thing, crossing all the t`s and dotting all the i`s. Believe me, after all our efforts, we were not going to fail due to some technicality! Within ten days everything was signed, sealed and posted to Sophie Whiting at Guinness World Records in London. Marie checked to see had they received the information, and was told that we had passed stage one of the examination, and that it was now down to the record verifiers, whether we had set a new world record or not. After more phone calls and faxes from Marie-it was too important and too close for me to ring-Ann Collins sent a fax verifying a new world record. It was verified on my birthday July 15th, and the cer-tificates arrived within a few days. Needless to say, all involved-and I think that included the whole of Galway-were delighted. Not many people can claim to have set a world record, and it is something that Francis Power and I will never forget and, hopefully, will always be remembered for doing!

Connacht Sentinel

Tennis World Record bid

Two members of the Galway Lawn Tennis Club will attempt to break the world record for continuous play by a doubles team. The record stands at 24 hours and 24 minutes. **Mike Geraghty** and will play tennis matches continually from 2 p.m. June 20 to 4 p.m. June 21. A replay of club members will take on Mike and Francis in a series of 3-set doubles matches.

There are strict criteria to obtain a world record. Independent witnesses must monitor and visually corroborate the attempt. Two stewards must be on duty at all times to ensure compliance with regulations. Breaks are limited to five minutes per hour and medical personnel must be available.

Mike and Francis are fit and looking forward to the challenge. The club has planned music, movies and a barbeque to keep player and spectators entertained and alert throughout the record attempt. The event will be run in aid of the Galway Mentally Handicapped Association.

Mike Geraghty and Francis Power of Galway Lawn Tennis Club tennis world record bid.

Daily Mirror

Tennis 2 to net record

By NIALL MOONAN

TWO tennis fanatics are set to smash a world record – by playing non-stop for 26 hours.

Galway Lawn Tennis club pals Mike Geraghty and Francis Power hope to break the previous record of 24 hours and 24 minutes.

They will start playing at 2pm this Friday and will continue until 4pm the following day.

A relay of club members will take on the pair in a series of three-set doubles matches.

Ball Girl Nicole ready to go

Nicole & Lee give dad a hand

16

Someday I'll be King
(Michael looks to future)

Sun in Galway a good omen

Lawrence of Arabia and Eminem

Now I Know how
Michael Schumacher feels

Galway duo set new world record in doubles tennis

BY SINEAD MCGOVERN

TWENTY SIX hours of play stretching from Friday at 2pm until Saturday at 4pm established a world record in doubles tennis for two members of the Galway Lawn Tennis Club, Mike Geraghty and Francis Power last weekend.

The event was monitored by three independent witnesses, 26 stewards, and more than 100 walk in witnesses in the 26 hours. The previous record held was for 24 hours and 24 minutes. Mike Geraghty, the original instigator behind the record attempt, said that they could have gone on even longer, "I thought 26 hours was a good time to set because a marathon is 26 miles. We could have gone on even longer, but we said that we'd stop when we had reached the 26 hour mark."

Geraghty, who owns the Video Library in Newcastle, first started thinking about making a record breaking attempt last August. "I rang up the *Guinness Book of Records* to find out what the existing record was. I decided that the temperature in mid summer would be perfect for it, then all I had to do was to find a lunatic to play with me." His partner in the successful attempt was 18-year-old Francis Power, who only joined the tennis club last May.

Obtaining a world record requires that strict criteria be adhered to, but Geraghty is confident that they did everything according to the rules. "We won't know for sure for another two or three weeks if we've made it into

• Mike Geraghty and Francis Power pictured with Mayor Val Hanley before they started last weekend.

the *Guinness Book of Records*, but we did everything by the book and recorded the match on video, and took loads of photographs so I'm pretty confident."

Geraghty, who reported no aches or pains in the slightest after the marathon tennis match, was delighted with the support they received. "It was fantastic. Everyone was so enthusiastic and gave us such great support. There were more than 70 club members there at the end."

The successful record attempt also doubled as a very successful fundraising event for the Galway Mentally Handicapped Association. More than €800 has been donated. However, Geraghty is determined to raise at least 1000 for the charity and has organised another carity event for this weekend. 'The fastest serve in the west', will begin at the tennis club at 2pm on Sunday. In search of 'the fastest serve in the west', there will be a charge of 1 for children and 2 for five serves. The speed of the serves will be measured by a speed gun. The current record in the tennis club for fastest serve is held by Tommy Hehir, who has a serve of 119 miles per hour. The event is open to members and non-memnbers.

Galway Advertiser

World Record before & after

18

Chapter 3

WORLD RECORD HOLDERS

Having played the 26 hours and received a lot of acclaim, Francis and I waited eagerly for confirmation of our world record. We felt like celebrating, but at the back of our minds, there remained a nagging doubt that GWR would find some reason not to declare us as world record holders. Marie Gordon was very positive and always stated, that " Everybody who was there knows you set a world record, and we did everything by the book, so there shouldn't be a problem." I love positive people, and Marie certainly comes into that category. She kept chasing GWR for confirmation, and finally they relented and sent a fax. We attended a club presentation, and President Pat Folan gave us GLTC tracksuits and lovely framed photographs of the two record setters and the Mayor. This was terrific and appreciated, but I have to say that not till I received my certificate, from the keeper of the records, did it feel real! The great thing was that we had created an entirely new world record. The information that I had been given by GWR was that there was a record of 24 hours 24 minutes, when in fact this referred to singles, so we created a record for the longest doubles match by one pair, taking on all-comers. Now, that was some achievement.

In mid-September 2003 the Irish Independent announced the publication of The Guinness Book of Records for 2004. Immediately I knew it was too soon, and with a May cut off date, we would not be in it. I rang my mother, who I knew would be in town, to check in Eason's, and she rang back to confirm my worst suspicions. She told me that as she went to check the book, two schoolboys were looking to see if Mike and Francis were in the book. The disappointment in their faces gave my Mum a glimpse of what Francis and I felt. The whole team were on a downer as we wondered would the record hold until the next publication. However in the same newspaper, an article about the Irish holding more world records per capita than any other country caught my attention. "There is a book in that" I told my friends, "and, I am going to write it". Over the next few months from time to time I would write a bit about it, and I compiled a scrapbook of our achievement. I checked a few times throughout the year with GWR, and each time our record still stood. In June 2004 I received a phone call from Scott Christie at GWR, inquiring would we be interested in hooking up with an American duo, who wanted to attempt breaking our record. You bet I was interested, but nothing came of the approach, because GWR would only forward our addresses and numbers to them, but would not furnish us with their details. I found this very strange and too secretive for my liking.

In August 2004 I received another call from GWR, to see would I speak with a journalist from the Examiner about our world record. "No worries, by the way will we be in the 2005 Edition?" I enquired. "Yes" replied the caller. I could not believe it; Francis and I were going to be in the 50th Anniversary Edition of Guinness Book of Records. What odds that we would be honoured in the edition marking 50 years since Roger Bannister (one of my Dad's idols) set a World Record for the first sub four-minute mile! I insisted that the lady check the book to be sure, and then began to inform the world, or at least Galway, of our achievement. The General Manager of GLTC, Siobhan Hawkins, contacted Galway Bay Fm and Keith Finnegan rang me up, live, for a chat. Oliver Martyn put out a press release, and all the local papers picked it up. GWR invited the two of us to The Gravity Bar in Dublin in November, to celebrate the book launch, and we met other record holders and signed copies of the book for kids. Francis remarked that the GWR people all knew my name; I'm sure that is because I kept hassling them to get permission to set up a record attempt. We met the fastest talking man in the world, and one of the GWR people remarked that on a good day I could give him a run for his money! Francis pointed out that most people in Galway spoke that quickly, and they should check it out. We got medals to mark our achievement, and I brought 3 extra for Michael, Lee and Nicole. All the back up team were delighted, however I did warn them that if anyone ever beat our record that I would be calling on them again. Little did they know how much I meant it!

Newcastle tennis players enter world records book

Two tennis player from Newcastle — who joined the unique club of world record holders on June 20-21 last year when they played the longest competitive doubles tennis match ever — have made it into the prestigious 50th anniversary edition of the Guinness World Records 2005.

Mike Geraghty and Francis Power joined the unique club of world record holders on June 20-21, 2003, creating a new world record for the longest competitive doubles tennis match for one pair playing against all comers. The match lasted approximately 26 hours at Galway Lawn Tennis Club.

The cut off point for new records was May in 2003, so even though their record has stood for 15 months to date, it debuts in the prestigious 50th anniversary edition of Guinness World Records 2005.

The two Galway men now feature alongside Andy Roddick, Martina Navratilova, Bjorn Borg and Goran Ivanisevic, among others, in the tennis section of the book. Naturally, the two Galway men are delighted, as at any given time there are 30,000 different records competing to feature in the annual production.

Given that the target readership of the annual is teenagers, both Mike and Francis expect that there will be many challenges to their record in the future. Indeed, at a time when Roger Federer is taking the men's game to a new level, this record proves anything is possible.

Francis Power and Mike Geraghty looking at their World Record entry in Guinness Book of World Records 2005.

Connacht Sentinel

Net prophets — Francis Power and Mike Geraghty of Galway Lawn Tennis Club pictured with the *2005 Guinness Book of Records* which features their record-breaking longest tennis game held at Galway Lawn tennis Club earlier this year.

Galway Advertiser

Chapter 4

RECLAIMING OUR WORLD RECORD

In May 2005 I rang GWR, to see if I could get some information on Irish World Record Holders for my book. Scott Christie informed me that they did not give access to these records, and they would not be in favour of publicising any one country as having more records per capita than any other. Displeased as I was to hear this, I asked him to check to see if our world record still stood. He really made my day by informing me that a pair from Germany now held the record, for the longest competitive doubles match by one pair against all-comers. Immediately I requested an application form to reclaim "our record". Scott informed me that it was all done online now, so I thanked him for his help and pondered on my next step.

On arriving home I called my three kids together. "Bad news guys, the world record has been broken by two German players. Will I leave it to them or get it back?" In unison Michael, Lee and Nicole shouted: "You have to get your record back Dad"! With support like, that how could I not reclaim it? I rang Francis and from then it was a matter of when, not if. Once Francis confirmed that he was ok for July 8th I rang Marie. I asked her if she remembered the promise she made, of helping us reclaim our record if it was broken. She didn't hesitate to offer full support. Marie had since married and moved from being Club Administrator at GLTC to 'The Treasure Chest', so she would not be able to be with us for the duration as in 2003, but she agreed to handle the paperwork, compile all the requirements for verification of the record, having set up a membership number and a claim number for the record attempt. Now here was the challenge: who would fill the Marie Gordon role of 2003? Who would be the glue to keep the plan together? I quickly guaranteed the support of my old committee: Gai Barry, Sinead Barry, Oliver Martyn and Nicky Nash. Thanks to Francis, we got three new members: Sheila Dempsey, Edwin Brennan and Sarah Caulfield.

Sheila has been head receptionist at GLTC for a long time. I first came across her when she played junior tennis and badminton. I remember she had a great left-handed smash, and had terrific sporting pedigree. Donal Snr I have mentioned before as the number one member of GLTC. In February 2004 I was delighted, as President of GLTC, to attend his 80th birthday party, and yes, he is still playing regularly. Ita, Sheila's mum, who sadly passed away in May 2003, did more for junior members of tennis and badminton over the years than you could imagine. Donal Jnr or 'Rigor', short for rigormortis for his minimum of movement on a tennis court, deserted the sport for hockey, but is still remembered as one of the last characters at the club, Sheila's sister Eimear must surely be one of the most talented racket players ever produced by Connacht. In all my four terms as Tennis Captain and my term as President, Sheila was a great support. Nothing was too much trouble, and when Francis told me that she was keen to help us I was delighted. From the start Sheila got totally involved, and at all times despite the demands Francis and I put on her she showed remarkable composure. Little did I know that we had found someone to step into Marie's shoes as our 'Girl Friday & Saturday,' that quickly. Edwin Brennan first came to my notice in December 2003. As I headed into the Club AGM seeking election as President, I met Edwin heading to the meeting. "How come you're going?" I asked, as you do not get too many juniors attending club AGMs. "I've come to vote for you" was his reply. With allies like this how could we fail? Sarah was just back from Australia, and had also been involved in 2003. On that occasion as you may remember she attended a Bon Jovi concert and then played in a world record attempt a few hours later. This time round Sarah was more involved in organising the event, and Francis had persuaded her to look after the bar for the Saturday night celebrations. What an optimist he was!

Originally I chose July 8th as the date for out attempt, and Marie confirmed this date with GWR. However this date clashed with the Connacht Open Veterans Tournament, and the feeling of the Tennis Committee was that our event would detract from the sponsor and the competition itself. In hindsight they were right, but it put us back a few weeks in our preparation. However it did allow more preparation time. Eventually we settled on Friday August 5th/Saturday 6th, which in a way was appropriate, as our original record had been broken the previous August. Marie liased with GWR, while Sheila was the focal point at the club; and she chased suppliers for water and chocolate, as well as making sure the court was in optimum condition. Francis and I started chasing sponsorship His dad, Geoff, persuaded BIG O Taxi Co, who he worked for, to sponsor us. Francis' cousins went door to door, and his brother Geoffrey got his friend Olly Raftery to DJ for the Saturday night. I persuaded the film companies I deal with, National Cable Vision Ltd and Sony Pictures to make a donation, and contacted a family friend Jackie Cunningham, to get his company, Jaycee Printers, to supply the donation cards. We both gave a lot of thought to the charity that would benefit from our world record attempt, and whereas originally I wanted to donate to an organisation involved in tackling obesity, we were unable to source any particular charity, and decided to do a joint event for Mark Griffin and University College Hospital Galway. Both Francis and I wanted to do something for children, so I contacted UCHG and selected the UCHG Children's fund, after speaking with Anne Matthews. Francis's brother Geoffrey was a friend of Mark Griffin, who had been involved in a road accident in Manchester and was receiving rehabilitation treatment in Dunleary, so on Francis' suggestion, we chose to do a joint event.

Our committee met just once and we went through all that had to be done. Oliver and Edwin would take care of Public Relations, I would invite the Mayor, Francis would sort out the social side of the event, Marie would oversee proceedings regarding all the paperwork, Sheila would double check everything from the club side and monitor players, stewards, medics etc, I would cover the physios and doctors, donation cards and contact Nicky re fruit and the clock, Gai would contact Galway Bay Fm and Sinead would do her usual job of helping with everything. Throughout the next few weeks there would be many phone calls and checks as we neared the big day. Ralph O' Gorman mentioned the upcoming attempt weekly, in the Galway Independent in his Sports shorts, and I did an interview with him on the preceding Monday. There was much more excitement all round this time. TV3 contacted me to say that barring a major news event they would film us before we started. However the story of the return of the Columbia 3 postponed our TV debut.

What amused me mostly was people's attitude to our attempt. In 2003 when we set a new world record, most people doubted that we would be able to last 26 hours; now nobody seemed to doubt it. I felt that people did not quite appreciate that we would be attempting to put 10 hours onto our previous record. Think about it: we were going to attempt to play competitive tennis for a day and a half, with accumulated physio breaks of 5 minutes per hour, no sleep, no real rest; I mean, how often have you stayed awake for that long, let alone stayed outside and competed in the most aerobic sport there is? On reflection, with the exception of watching Andre Agassi at the U.S. Open night matches a couple of times, I don't think I have ever been wide awake at dawn, and this would be the second time in two years we were going to do it. Whatever about the general public, Francis and I were aware of the extra effort that we would have to put in to achieve our goal. Some even asked would we do more than 36 hours. Francis answered swiftly "Mike will probably want to but I'm stopping at Midnight"! That put an end to that discussion.

On the three or four days leading up to the event I felt mentally tired. This surprised even Michelle, who when I frequently mentioned it would reply, "But you're never tired". In hindsight I think that, psychologically, I was preparing myself to make Court 7 my office for 36 hours, and even if I had to have an intravenous drip attached to my arm and crawl round that court, I would complete the target 36 hours. I spoke to Francis the night before our attempt to see how he was feeling. He told me that he had felt a bit nervous leading up to it, but now felt fine. I don't believe that on either occasion, either of us doubted that the other one would be up for the task ahead, and knowing the characters, I know that neither of us ever doubted ourselves. The same evening we both did phone interviews with the Irish Times, and both fielded many text messages wishing us luck over the two days. That Monday I had sent a letter to my two friends Maura Grealish and Marina Hayden in the Poor Clare's Convent, asking them to not only say a prayer for us themselves, but to get all the sisters to mount a vigil for us throughout the 36 hours. Little did I know that Ger Brennan, my doctor and one of the key players in ensuring our health throughout both attempts, had asked the same favour of the nuns. Ger's secretary, Anne, had again got him to sign a certificate of good health for me to compete, even if he still maintains that it was Anne who added mentally sound as well as physically fit-something he says he could not stand over. At least he was consistent, because when I asked him to help us in 2003 he told me it was psychiatric help that we would need, not medical, if we were going to try and play 26 hours of tennis.

I went to bed at 10 pm and read the papers before getting a good night's sleep-rested and ready for the journey ahead. Roy Keane's motto of "Fail to Prepare, Prepare to Fail" is one I live by. In the preceding weeks I had spoken with Brian McGoldrick, Ger Brennan, Rita Halloran-who, like Ger, would be checking on us throughout the 36 hours as she had done in 2003-and Erin Ryan, who had been one of our physios on call in 2003. Erin was brilliant this time round. She organised all of the physios, and we had many more on duty this time, because I felt that we were very fortunate to escape injury in 2003. First time round we had both experienced cramp and minor injuries. This time I wanted to lessen the damage of cramping, by having rubdowns every six hours with physios on call on a four-hour rota. Erin organised all this for me. What a weight off my mind to know that between Ger, Rita and Erin we would be in very safe hands. Too much was at stake to fail through lack of planning.

I spoke with Erin about what we ate and drank the last time. She advised me to lower the sugar intake and get more salt into the system. I switched my drinking from the magic mix of 7-up and water to Robinson's Orange Barley Water, diluted with water. This is what I always drink when I'm playing matches and even at home with meals etc. I brought Tuc biscuits for the salt intake, as Michelle correctly reasoned that I would not drink the orange if it were mixed with salt. She may think that I put too high a price on achievement, but she does know me better than anyone else. On Ger's advice I decided to eat more than the last time. We went on the principle that if "When you're thirsty it's too late to start drinking, the damage is already done," that the same should apply to eating. So Francis and I would generally keep nibbling throughout the 36 hours, preventing ever getting really hungry. Francis can take a lot of different foods to me, and was able to eat pasta and such like first time round, while I relied on bananas, chocolate and rice crispies. This time round I decided to bring pitta bread with ham, and Michelle would replenish the supplies as I got through them. If there was anything we had forgotten, we knew that Sheila, Sarah, Edwin and Michelle would track it down for us. Again, once we hit the court we did not want to have to worry about anything. However, even this theory would be put to the test at 7.30 on the Friday night!

Chapter 5

THE LONGEST DAY (AND A HALF)!

Friday August 5th 2005 began very much like June 20th 2003. The sun was out and the clear blue sky augured well for the task ahead. I had just finished breakfast when Nicky turned up as promised, with the fruit and the clock. Talk about Mr Reliable! There were enough bananas to keep Dublin Zoo going for 36 hours, never mind two tennis players. He also brought grapes and satsumas. Nicky was full of encouragement, and was scheduled to play against us from 10 to 12 pm both nights. I eased into the day and we collected Francis, as we did in 2003, arriving at the club at 11am. Sheila and Edwin were there to welcome us and the independent witnesses arrived shortly after. Frank, Brendan and Michael were set for another long journey, but we could see that they were well prepared. After a few checks that all was in order, we went onto court 7 to knock up. We could immediately see the difference there was a great press presence this time round. There were freelance photographers as well as the Nationals and a journalist from the Irish Times.

Our first opponents were Frances & Helen Sheehan, and at 12 noon Helen opened the proceedings by acing Francis with her first serve. I hoped it wasn't an omen! We were delighted to get such a lively opener, as you never know how people will react when they are partaking in a world record attempt. The two sisters provided a nice upbeat start to the event. Francis and I eased into our first match, and cruised through five straight sets, including a knock with local councillor Niall O'Brolchain and Club Champion Marion Hanley. I had asked Niall would he come to the record attempt and hit a few balls, and he was delighted to take up our offer. He showed some promise and Brian McGoldrick tried to get him to join the club. Niall would feature prominently in our efforts later, and if his enthusiasm on a tennis court is matched in the political field he will go far.

Francis and I decided that we would play until 6pm without a break, so we would aggregate time for a physio rubdown, and always have some time to spare in case we needed it later. We kept drinking and eating at the 90-second breaks, and the weather was so good it was a joy to stay on court. The second match featured Brian McGoldrick and Oliver Martyn. Brian had umpired the first match, and he and Oliver were up for this match. We made a quick start, as we were well warmed up, and took the first set, 6-0. However the two lifted their game - remember Brian is a regular opponent of ours on Thursday nights - and Oliver really upped his game and was drilling the ball round the court. The second set went to a tiebreak and, compared to the first match, seemed to go on a long time. We negotiated the breaker, and took the third set, 6-3. We had now played for four hours and next up were Gerard Brennan and Gavin Melody. I was delighted that these two new additions to our now expanded Thursday night doubles group were teaming up to play us. The lads loved the big occasion-bit of a crowd building, and some entertaining umpiring from Marion Hanley and then Emma Murphy, ably assisted by Aoife Forde. This match also saw the introduction of ball girls Maria, Bronagh and Aoife. They soon got the hang of feeding the server, and moving the tennis balls round the court at speed. They were a great help, and I'm sure they all enjoyed being part of history! We even had celebratory guests! Gerard's uncle, Brendan Bowyer, accompanied by wife, Stella and daughter, Aisling turned up to cheer Gerard and Gavin on. Brendan was one of the biggest stars of the 'Showband Era', and moved to America where he has had even more success. Thankfully nobody prevailed on him to perform "the Hucklebuck" as he was enjoying the tennis too much to be working. We ran through four quick sets with the lads, and next up was to be a showcase match with two of the Tuesday doubles crew Mark Smyth and Daniel Cluskey.

At 6pm, after six hours play, I had a rubdown, and physio Jane Tormey worked on my lower back and my left calf, which was a bit tight. I had felt the calf injury from early in the afternoon, but you tend to know your own body and I was confident that it would respond to regular physio. Francis declined physio and had something to eat instead. The centrepiece of the evening was to be the Mayor's appearance at 7 pm, and so it was fitting that one of our best matches should be in full flow at this stage. However, after the break Francis and I were a bit flat, and the boys were hitting a great ball, obviously enjoying playing before a crowd. We dropped the first two sets 2-6, 2-6, and at this point my mind, in particular, was drifting to the whereabouts of the Mayor. During one of our 90-second turnovers, I got a mobile and rang Niall O'Brolchain to see would he deputise for the Mayor, as City Hall was closed and it was now approaching 8pm. Niall assured me that he would not let us down, and if he could not contact Brian Walsh he would deputise for him. Relieved that this was in hand, we finished off our third set with Mark and Dan, but it was our poorest performance of the day. A few minutes after speaking to Niall, I received a call from Mayor Brian Walsh. The council had told him 8.30pm instead of 7 pm, and he apologised for the delay but would be there at 8.30, if we still wanted him. Terrific-we were back on schedule, and started our next match with an Eastern European flavour. Tomas Dobrowski and Lobus Valdavek were our 8-10 pm opponents. We started the match and took the first set 6-2, breaking for a few minutes only when Mayor Brian Walsh arrived, for three photos. The first roll call was for Club President Garry O' Lochlainn, Tennis Captain Anne McGarry and Squash Captain Matt O' Connor; next up the team behind the team: Marie, Sheila, Edwin, Sarah, Gai, Sinead, Oliver, Frank and Brendan. Unfortunately Michael Needham, for a change, was not here-he was very vigilant in both attempts, but I suppose he had to go home the odd time. The third picture featured Mayor Walsh in the umpire's chair, flanked by Francis and myself. We thought that it would make a great entry for caption corner, but unfortunately the Galway Advertiser did not print it. I was delighted Brian could make it, as he is very Sports minded, and very enthusiastic towards young people. Fair play to Niall for calling him at home and putting our minds at ease. We proceeded to win in three straight sets and at 10 pm Nicky Nash and Magz Wilson turned up to play us.

It was dark now and the accompanying charity event to raise funs for CROI, organised by Diana Hogan-Murphy, was coming to an end. This meant that there would be a big crowd for a while, and as we neared mid-night the numbers would dwindle. We would soon enter the period where you had to keep your mind extra active, and stave off mental tiredness, as well as physical tiredness. We had been there before, which was a big help. It's amazing the amount of people who came to see us over the 36 hours. I asked those who hadn't been out to the club before, to come over and let us know that they had come out to see us, and I'm delighted to report that they didn't let me down. Most of these came on Saturday; they had all asked, "When should we come out to see you?" and I told them all Saturday; because I felt that we would need the boost more, then, than on the Friday. Michelle and the kids came out after 9pm, and her mum Edith came out with her partner, Jack Gunning shortly after. I knew my mother-in-law was present when I heard her shout, "Come on Mike," and put some life into the crowd. There was a carnival atmosphere and Francis was enjoying the banter with the crowd, as he knew his friends, Ciaran Gilchrist and Carl Falsey, would be playing us at 2am, and I knew that was the match he was looking forward to most. The only match I contemplated was the present one, knowing that we would be playing against Nicky again in 24 hours, on the final leg (hopefully not literally) of our journey. We had played against Nicky and Magz on many occasions, and knew that this would be a good test. The first set was tight. We nicked it 7-5 before motoring away 6-0 in the second and it was going with serve 3-4 in the third set when midnight struck.

We took a break at 12, and I got another rubdown. This time the physio was my friend Erin Ryan, who had organised all the physios for us. Erin was full of encouragement, as she had been when watching us in 2003. She worked on my back and the troublesome calf, which she said was quite tight but I would be able to play through it. While she saw Francis, I had one of the many pittas that Michelle had left for me, and spoke with some of the team. Edwin was filming a few minutes of every match, and Sheila and Sarah were making sure that we had everything we needed. Without this type of dedication it would have been much harder for Francis and myself to get through the task ahead. We were both totally confident that we had a great back-up team looking after us. Ger Brennan and Rita Halloran were in and out throughout the whole period; checking on us and making sure we were in tip-top condition. Even though she had said she would not be around as much as in 2003, Marie Gordon was constantly checking that operations were proceeding smoothly, and again the tennis club was like a second home to a very dedicated lady.

I can't emphasise enough how much of a team effort this was. Francis and I were the visible tip of the iceberg, but a lot of preparation goes into attempting world records. That is why we were both very particular in who we wanted with us. I would back that team to accomplish anything, and I was proud to work with them. I still find it hard to believe that all of those who had been involved in our first world record didn't even hesitate before committing to help us attempt to reclaim our record. I know Marie will tell you that I elicited this response out of them all by reminding them all that they had agreed to it back in 2003 after our first record was verified! The midnight match featured Sinead Barry and Eimear Hardiman, another friend of Francis' who had been on a coaching course with him. There were some good exchanges on court, and we eased our way through three sets in anticipation of our next match.

2 am was an unusual time for the showpiece match of the event "The World Record Holders for the Longest Singles Match versus The Potential World Record Holders for the Longest Doubles Match, by one pair taking on all-comers". This was Francis' idea and it was just what we needed. People constantly ask me "Were you not tired?" and I can honestly say that the only time I felt tired was for a twenty minute period from about 2-2.20 am on that Saturday morning. That's probably because I would be normally fast asleep at that time. It was getting colder now as the temperatures dropped, and the mist and damp weather that would accompany us for much of our journey until around 4pm in the afternoon was beginning to fall. The lads, Ciaran and Carl, were good-much bigger hitters than we had encountered, with the exception of Mark and Dan, - and the banter started with the first point. These guys were determined to enjoy their weekend in Galway-as was Eimear, who umpired and commentated, keeping us all going as the night wore on-but they also came to play tennis. We took the first set 6-4, the lads got some momentum in the second and took it 6-2, the third was a cliffhanger, with the boys edging it 7-5. We definitely lost our way in the fourth, dropping it 6-1; however we had the upper hand in the fifth, serving a break up at 5-4, when Carl had to take an injury time out, and get treatment on a shoulder injury. It had occurred in one of our long all-court rallies. After cross courting from backhand to backhand, Carl approached the net at speed and I threw up a topspin backhand lob into the far corner of the court. Unfortunately on a now greasy surface, Carl slipped and came down on his shoulder. He bravely played on, even switching hands at times, but as dawn neared he knew there was no point in causing further harm to the injury, and decided to stop as soon as our physio, the bright eyed Erin Ryan, arrived. She was a busy lady; Ciaran's shoulder; Francis' shoulder was now beginning to play up, and my calf was in need of a good rub by now!

When we returned to court, Edwin Brennan and Ger Flaherty arrived with the dawn chorus. Ger was another member of our back-up medical team, and I can vividly remember him umpiring our match with Ciaran and Carl, as at one point he joined the now ever present and bubbly Eimear, Francis, the two lads and myself, in one of our changeover breaks to eat Tuc biscuits. Ger was very impressed at my initiative in getting salt into the system, and enjoyed the witty exchanges, where such weighty subjects as best book written on tennis, worst ever Irish manager etc. were debated. Edwin, who I now firmly believe lives in the tennis club, and certainly never left it before, during, or in the immediate aftermath of our marathon, played a set with us which we took, 6-3, and then to fit him in, they graciously allowed Neil McLoughlin to partner Eimear against us for a set. Again, we must have been conserving energy, as we trailed 6-1, before upping our game to lead, 2-0, in the second set, before our 8 am opponents arrived. During our 8-10 am slot, at Francis' insistence, we all ordered out for breakfast rolls. I think it was Edwin who got them. In 2003 I could not contemplate eating such a heavy meal, but I was determined to keep my energy levels up, and gave in to the temptation of sausage, rashers, mushroom and egg, with tomato ketchup in a roll. I swore not to eat for a further six hours, and I'm pretty sure it was at least that long before I ate again. I remember Tommy Hehir putting on the Bar-B-Q, to keep everybody warm, and Margaret McLoughlin turning up with a flask of tea, as promised, even though I barely got to drink half a cup throughout the day. We had an enjoyable match with Diana Hogan-Murphy and Thereze Waldron next. There was a very entertaining exchange between Diana and umpire, Eimear, who referred to Diana as "Blondie" throughout the match, and slagged off Thereze about Mayo or "Mayooo" as she called it. I had been fortunate to partner both our opponents, and reached semi-finals with both in recent years, so we knew we would have a good match with the ladies. We got a bit careless, dropping the first set 6-4, obviously down to Francis' injured shoulder, but stormed back to take the second, 6-4, and lead 3-0, in the third, before our time ran out.

The match that provided the most laughs was the 10 am match with Francis's brother Geoffrey and Olly Raftery. I had spoken with Geoffrey the previous week, and he thought that after 24 hours on court we might be tired, and they would have a chance. He had said that we were probably twenty times fitter than they were, so I pointed out that after 24 hours on court we would still probably be 5 times fitter than them! Francis wanted to annihilate the pair, whereas I wanted to relax a bit, play a few drop volleys, and move the boys round the court a little. It made quite a spectacle! Geoffrey and Olly chased down ball after ball, while Francis tried to inflict as much pain as possible on them, and I generally surprised them by killing a lot of shots dead with stop volleys. The first two sets we cruised along, 6-1, 6-1. In the third set the lads were getting into it and it was closer, 6-4.

We took another physio break at mid-day. To save time Sharon Morris, who had also been on duty in 2003, worked on both of us at the same time. We were vigilant in sticking to the time, as we were allowed five minutes for every hour played, and we decided to use the bulk of this time for physio. Sharon gave my back a thorough going over, as the calf wasn't too bad now, and she concentrated on Francis' shoulder and neck. In fairness to Francis, due to a shoulder injury, he had been unable to serve flat-out since early on the Saturday morning, even if his under-arm was sufficiently difficult for our opponents to break. I decided then that he could avail of the rest of our allocated physio treatment, as I was confident that I would be fine from thereon in whereas, to keep him going I knew that Francis would need plenty of treatment on the shoulder and neck.

We were both a little out of sorts going into our next match against Donal Hegarty and Barry O' Donovan, two long term friends of mine. I started the current Club Champion, Donal, playing tennis in 1990, and he has had a brilliant senior tennis career, winning the club championship twice, the Connacht Open O-35 singles, and representing Connacht at senior and veteran Inter-provincial Level. We were finalists in the O-35 Doubles one year and won the Plate another time; also he we have both played together for the Connacht O-35 team for the last few years. Barry and I have known each other since I started playing tennis at GLTC in 1982, and we set up a tennis club in the "Jes", the school we both attended, when I was teaching and Barry was doing his Leaving Cert. I would have preferred to have competed against this pair when we were both a bit fresher, but I think after fairly intensive physio treatment, Francis and I were a bit off our game in this match. Also I believe that at this period Francis was getting a bit tired mentally. This was to be expected, as it's bound to hit you sometime when you undertake something as arduous as we did. I had felt mentally tired, as I mentioned before, in the days leading up to our world record attempt, but mentally I was perfectly attuned to the task at hand. In hindsight I think Francis had concentrated more on organising the social side of the event, playing against his friends from Dublin, and the celebrations after. That is fine too and, it's a necessary distraction, but at some time the enormity of it all hits you and that's when it weighs heavy on your mind and body. If there is a "wall," then mentally this is it. I had headed this off by thinking about what it would entail, earlier in the week. The lads raced into a 5-0 lead, and we were mortified as we found it hard to get into the match. They were playing very well, and we were both making lots of errors. Typical-as the crowd built up we seemed to be fading. Luckily with a combination of Barry and Donal easing off, and the pair of us lifting our game, we pulled back three games as they closed out the set, 6-3. They played out of their trees to take the second set, 6-0, and we got another lease of life to take the third, 6-3. There were some great rallies in the third set as everyone hit top form. It was like a throwback to the early nineties, to chase round the court competing against Barry and Donal, as if everything depended on each point.

At 2pm Colette Murphy, a star ball girl at both world record attempts, teamed up with Rita Halloran, obviously needing to check up close if her two patients were up to the task. It was during this match that we experienced our mini-crisis. I popped over for a quick chat with the crowd during a changeover break, and Michelle said that Francis had indicated that he would not be able to do the 36 hours. I am sure that anybody who knows me can imagine my thoughts on hearing this. Ger Brennan was watching at the time, and he was concerned that Francis looked tired. I brushed off their concern, but sure enough, shortly after, Francis told me that he might not complete the 36 hours, but felt that he could play on until we broke the record of 33hours, 33 minutes and 33 seconds. They say forewarned is forearmed, so I calmly told him to see how he felt, and we could decide later. At the next changeover I enlisted the help of the crowd. I told the younger supporters like Emma and Aoife to pass it around: "Cheer Francis"; every time he hits a ball shout, "Come on Francis", not to mind me, because I was totally motivated. I had a word with his dad, Geoff. Geoff, a former Garda, and friend of my dad, was now driving a taxi, but this would go on hold now as he would support Francis through to the end, and what support he provided. I can still hear him shouting, "Francis, I did three days duty without sleep when the Pope was here in 1979 and surely you can hit tennis balls for 36 hours." Whether it made him mad or motivated him I don't know, but Francis kept working. My mum, Florrie, had brought her cousin Fred and his family, who were on holiday from Wales, out to see us, and Heather, his daughter-in-law, got kit-kats for both of us, as she felt that a quick energy boost might help Francis. What Francis found hardest was to stay motivated in matches where the ball was not being hit hard and we could drift through easily. No disrespect to any of our opponents, but the balance was important, as no one could play full-out the whole time, and some of these matches were just what was needed to ease us through to the tougher battles ahead. This was easier for me to appreciate at the time, and I'm sure Francis feels the same in hindsight. We rolled nicely into our 4pm match with Felim Cluskey and Dympna Ormonde. This was the match that got us back on track. The first set was up and down with lots of service breaks, but after a few great rallies with an enthusiastic crowd playing their part we nicked it, 7-5. Felim and Dympna were revelling in the atmosphere and really lifted their games. We took the second set, 6-2, and were at 2-2 in the third when the bells chimed for 6pm.

I declined physio and Francis availed of a good rubdown, as I sat courtside chatting with Barry O' Donovan who, as well as playing against us earlier, was doing cover as a medic and a steward. Barry was always a great man for multi-tasking, so its good to see that nothing has changed on that front. Throughout the event people came out specially to see us, and Myles Monaghan who works with me at Newcastle Video Library popped out a couple of times, as did Conal Whitmarsh, Gabriel D'Arcy with his sons Dion and Gabriel, and David and Imelda Hickey. Paul and Fiona Griffin supported us in both marathons, and Michael McNeela (my campaign manager in the 2004 Local Elections) was there to add his support. It was a terrific boost to see them all, and it brought home to me how big the whole event was. Francis and I had certainly turned this into a far more public event than our original world record in 2003. My left instep was a bit sore, due no doubt to the fact that I had been wearing tennis shoes for nearly a day and a half at this stage, so I applied an ice pack for a couple of minutes during the break.

Gai and Sinead Barry were next up, and this was a nice match to ease along our journey. Two of our committee, the Barry ladies, have become great friends and accomplices of mine over the years. When I finished my fourth Tennis Captaincy in 2000 I told Gai that we would team up again in future, and I am positive she never doubted it. The call came in November 2002 when I was running an "Open Day" for the Tennis Club. The President, Pat Folan, asked me would I organise such an event, and I made Marie Gordon and Gai Barry my first two calls. Needless to say it was a success, and we had a bit of fun too. In January 2003 I persuaded Gai to seek election to the Board of Directors alongside Donal Hegarty and myself, and we were all successful in our bid. Gai did a terrific job as P.R.O., and her newsletter from the spring of 2003 to January 2005 was a great success, and kept club members up to date on what was happening - good and bad. Sinead, as mentioned earlier, is an intrinsic part of any event that I have been associated with over the last few years. Sinead even joined me on the campaign trail in the Local Elections in 2004. We had a bit of fun and relaxed in this match, as the crowd began to grow.

Next up were former Club President Pat Folan and Ladislav Visnevsky. It was during this match that I got the news I had been wishing for; Francis told me that he was going to play until midnight and complete the 36 hours. It was all systems go now! We raced through the match in great style, and for the second time Pat Folan was on a court when a World Record was set. We stopped for a few minutes at 9.34pm, just as we broke the existing record set in Germany 12 months previously! Francis and I went into the crowd to be greeted by a really enthusiastic group, and as happened two years previously the members came out of the woodwork. Michelle, Michael, Lee and Nicole were there to see the record reclaimed. I hope in years to come my kids will feel as proud as I was at that moment. Making history once is a good feeling, but second time round is even more satisfying. There is an old saying that I firmly concur with: " Winning or achieving something is great, but losing what you had and regaining it is far more satisfying." People were genuinely excited and delighted at our achievement, but now we were entering unchartered territory, extending the record to 36 hours.

The last match was one that we were both looking forward to all day. Nicky Nash, my great friend and ally, and Tommy Hehir, another player that I started off playing tennis, who came back to haunt me, would be our last test. You could not pick a better finale. These guys played a big part in both World Record attempts, and now would be the last players to take us on in our "Uber-Marathon". Since a marathon is 26 miles; or originally in our case 26 hours-and the fact that we were reclaiming our title from a German pair, I coined the phrase "uber marathon" or super marathon, as we had gone beyond the marathon. Fittingly, this was the best match of the event. With a capacity crowd cheering on our every shot, all four of us got into it big time. We took the first set, 6-3, including what seemed like a twenty-minute service game of mine, which we finally held. At one point the whole thing seemed surreal to me. It was as if I was looking in at the match and the whole court from a different place. For one moment the crowd seemed distant, the ball girls Emma, Aoife and Elaine appeared to be further away than I expected, and then suddenly I was back in a cross-court rally with Nicky. The lads took the second set, 6-3, and on Francis' insistence we took our last break of the match, to use up unexpired time we had accumulated. It was a short break but long enough for more well-wishers to come up to us. Eamonn Bradshaw M.B.E., former Club President, congratulated us both-along with Olwyn Raftery, Past President of Tennis Ireland and GLTC, Margaret McLoughlin-incomparable when it comes to working for junior tennis, Councillor Niall O Brolchain a great supporter during this event, Mickey "Little Sport" Walshe, longest serving President at GLTC and alongside Donal Dempsey (yes, of course he was there), one of the cornerstones, or should I say net-posts, of Galway Lawn Tennis Club-to name but a few. We took to the court for the last time in the marathon and, cheered on by a vocal crowd, allied to increasingly loud music from upstairs courtesy of Olly Raftery, along with shouts of "Come on Mike, Lets go Franny," we raced through to match point at 5-3, final set. As mid night beckoned the lads fended off three or maybe four match points. Finally as the clock struck 12 and GLTC erupted like never before, we nailed match point. GAME, SET, MATCH AND NEW WORLD RECORD!

Olly played "We are the champions" by Queen, and Mike Shaughnessy was there, fair play to him, to immortalise the moment on film. Will there ever be a more poignant moment in the history of GLTC? The crowd flocked down to congratulate us. I have never had so many handshakes and hugs, or seen the genuine look of awe in so many faces. If one or two people thought that they could play 26 hours after our previous exploits, I don't believe that anyone in GLTC believes that they could top 36! To paraphrase an infamous radio announcer, "Calling Germany; your record is smashed," "Ich bin ein Berliner" becomes "Is Eireannach Muid go leir!" To all of those other record breakers in history, from Roger Bannister to Richard Donovan, we salute you for inspiring us.

As much as I would have liked to head home, I knew the inevitable speech would have to be made in the bar. Francis hit the showers in anticipation of partying away the night, while I went up to the bar with Nicky and Anne McGarry, for a few sips of a 7-up. As "Simply the Best" echoed around the dance floor, a reluctant Francis and I made our way to the microphone. Surprisingly, my accomplice left the talking to me, and I made a brief speech, informing the crowd that as I was a bit knackered, I would probably forget to mention some people. So I briefly thanked my committee and announced my departure. Francis' mother told me the next day that he had half a beer and headed off shortly after. I think we were both entitled to go home at that stage. Mission accomplished!

You need 'cojones' of steel
to accomplish this

"And I thought Council meetings
went on along time".

Paparazzi everywhere

Nice of Ronaldo to show up for
Newcastle

War of the Worlds, survival of the
fittest. World record for Singles verses
World record for Doubles

The 'A Team' with Mayor Brian Walsh
deputising for Michael Needham

Serving up a world record bid

Irish Independent

Brian McDonald

TWO men are hoping to hear the magic words, "game, set and new record" just after midnight tonight, signalling that they have reclaimed the title of longest tennis doubles match in the history of the sport.

Video store owner, Mike Geraghty (43) and professional tennis coach, Francis Power (20), from Galway, yesterday began the quest to get their names back into the Guinness Book of Records.

Two years ago, they established the record for a doubles match at 26 hours, but this was surpassed last year by a German pair, who went on to play for 33 hours, 33 minutes and 33 seconds.

After several weeks of training and following a closely-monitored diet, the pair are attempting to play for 36 hours. Three independent monitors will see that they comply with the specific rules. A total of 36

Francis Power and Mike Geraghty of the Galway Lawn Tennis Club practising before their attempt at beating the world doubles record yesterday. Picture: Andrew Downes

experienced tennis players have signed up to provide the opposition - in two-hour stints - for the duration of the record attempt.

The duo began their assault on the new target figure at midday on a flood-lit court in Salthill yesterday. They are entitled to a five-minute break after every hour, but played straight through the first six hours to earn a half-hour meal break.

"We reckon that cramp could be the biggest threat to our attempt to win back the record," said Mike. "When we set the record in

2003, cramp struck after only about eight hours, but we managed to get by, that's why the physios are so important this time."

He added: "The lack of sleep shouldn't be a real problem as it is hard to fall asleep when you are active outdoors."

Game, set, match - and a world record

BY LINLEY MACKENZIE

Galway tennis players Mike Geraghty and Francis Power (above) have set a new world record for playing doubles tennis.

Last weekend at the Galway Lawn Tennis Club the pair played non-stop for 36 hours, playing against 18 different partnerships in two-hour stints.

Geraghty and Power had first broken the record in June 2003 when playing for 26 hours. However a German duo then set a new record of 33 hours, 33 minutes, and 33 seconds. That record had stood until Sunday

when the Galway players set about recapturing the record when they started at 12 noon on Friday. By 9.34pm on Saturday they had overtaken the Germans' time, but they continued until midnight to extend the time to 36 hours.

Along the way Power suffered a shoulder injury, while persistent rain on Saturday did not help their cause.

The two had a variety of opponents to play - including players from Sligo, Dublin, and Slovenia. World record holders for continuous singles tennis, Carl Falsey and Ciaran Gilchrist also travelled to Galway and provided the pair with a four-hour five-set match

between 2am and 6am on Sarturday morning. The Mayor of Galway, Brian Walsh, and Cllr Niall Ó'Brolcháin also lent their support, along with two doctors Ger Brennan and Rita Fennell, and a team of volunteer physios lead by Erin Ryan.

Geraghty, who is a video shop owner, says their success was due to their preparations - "regular exercise and plenty of water". However, he says, one of the strongest motivations was raising money for their two nominated charities at the same time, the Mark Griffin Fund and UCHG children's fund. To date some €1,500 has been raised by family and friends of the duo.

In addition to an organising committee, spearheaded by Marie Gordon and Sheila Dempsey, the pair had three independent witnesses, Frank Hayden, Michael Needham, and Brendan Kelly to ratify their achievements.

"A lot of behind the scenes work was done, and we would like to thank everyone, including those who acted as stewards, players, ball boys and girls, and those involved in catereing for the event which has attracted considerable publicity."

Donations can still be made in the Tennis Club 091-522353 or Newcastle video library 091-525022.

Galway Advertiser

Friday, July 29, 2005   Galway City Tribune

Mike Geraghty and Krawlis Power, who will be attempting a world record bid at Galway Lawn Tennis Club on August 5th and 6th.

Geraghty and Power aim to reclaim world record

TWO years ago Galway Lawn Tennis players Mike Geraghty and Francis Power created a new world record for playing 26 hours doubles in the longest competitive match against all comers. Subsequently a German pair posted a new record time of 33 hours, 33 minutes and 33 seconds, but between Friday, August 5th, at noon and Sat-

urday, August 6th, at midnight the Galway players will attempt to reclaim their place as world record holders.

The event will be a joint fund-raiser for the Children's Hospital at University College Hospital Galway and the Mark Griffin Fund.

Donations can be made at Galway Lawn Tennis Club or

to the two players.

To ensure the success of the event the players will need the help of Physios, Doctors, Stewards, independent witnesses, Umpires, Ball boys and girls as well as opponents.

If individuals want to sponsor the event or make a donation contact Francis 091-522353 or M 091-525022.

Galway City Tribune

Galway Independent

World-record breakers

Francis Power and Mike Geraghty photographed before their world-record-breaking attempt.
Galway Lawn Tennis Club members Francis Power and Mike Geraghty reclaimed their world record for playing doubles tennis nonstop for 36 hours and will now have their names re entered in the Guinness Book of Records. They started at 12 noon on Friday at the Galway Lawn Tennis Club and finished on Saturday at midnight. The independent witnesses Brendan Kelly, Frank Hayden and Michael Needham supervised Geraghty and Power play against 18 partnerships including Ciaran Gilchrist and Karl Falsey from Dublin who hold the world singles record at 30 hours! Gilchrist and Falsey played Geraghty and Power from 2.00am to 6.00am on Saturday morning (in the rain!). Marie Gordon administered the effort and Sheila Dempsey handled the logistics. All proceeds go to the Mark Griffin Fund and the UCHG Children's Fund. *Photo by Reg Gordon*

Galway Sentinel

Galway Lawn Tennis Club members Francis Power (left) and Mike Geraghty who broke the World doubles tennis playing record at the weekend. Photo: Joe O'Shaughnessy.

Chapter 6

BACK ON TOP OF THE WORLD

The day after we completed our second tennis marathon, I decided to take it easy and relax, reading the paper before rising to watch Leeds United open their promotion campaign on TV. However the phone rang around ten, and it was Lorna Siggins from the Irish Times, seeking an interview. No worries, I was only too delighted to update her on our successful negotiation of our second world record. My mobile was buzzing with congratulatory texts, and it being an older model, I had to delete them as I read them to get to the next text. I sent out a few more to a few friends who may not have heard, though this was unnecessary, as it seems like everyone had followed our progress this time! After enjoying a 2-0 Leeds victory, I decided to try and catch forty winks, but no sooner had my head hit the pillow than the phone rang. Oliver Martyn, our chief PRO, wondered would I do an interview, so he could prepare a press release for the papers. I bet Francis wasn't taking calls and they were all chasing me! I rang his home in the evening and spoke with his mother, who said that he and Neil had headed out to celebrate with some friends but that he was fine. I finally went to bed around 12.30 that night, but was up for work bright and early next morning.

Monday was a crazy day! No sooner had I opened the Video Library, than I had a call from Carmella Maffeo from the City Tribune, to do an interview for the Sentinel and Tribune. This took forty minutes and she was very thorough, contacting Francis straight after for his views. Edwin was on the phone updating me on what papers we were in, and any other requests they had at the club for information about our attempt. Edwin really thrived on his involvement and was fantastic support, making daily visits to the Video Library with newspaper and radio updates, and he could not have been more helpful. Sheila kept constant phone contact, and told me that it was very hard to get used to the quietness in the club, as there had been such excitement and activity in the days leading up to the marathon, and needless to say the club was buzzing with members old and new, as we reclaimed our record. Marie was outstanding at ensuring that we compiled all the press items, and that all the records of attendance were meticulously maintained and treble checked. Sheila and Sinead had been extremely thorough in filling in all the details, and nothing was going to be left to chance. Gai and I had set up a bank account for the joint charity event, and the money was coming in from Francis' relatives' canvassing of Corrib Park, to the Tennis Club and to the Video Library. This time it was better, as people came in to talk about our achievement and, more often than not, made donations on the spot.

Monday afternoon I brought the kids bowling with my mum Florrie and her cousins from Wales, who had supported us vigilantly on Saturday. Again the mobile was buzzing and a radio station from Cork, Red F.M., asked would I do a live interview that night about setting the world record. Before I went back to work that night I did a phone interview with the Galway Independent, and then met Oliver, who called in for me to see which photos he would send to the press. Francis had gone back to Dublin to work, so I was happy to wrap things up on this end. At 10.30 Red F.M. rang me at home, and I did a live interview with Victor who was amazed at our feat. The next day Edwin arrived with all the papers. Our interviews with Carmella appeared in a page-long feature in the Galway Sentinel. The previous day we were in the Irish Times, The Irish Independent and The Irish Examiner, as well as headlining the local news on Galway Bay FM. Imagine my delight at turning on the radio to hear the news that two Galway men have re-entered the Guinness Book of Records, by establishing a new world record of 36 hours tennis, battling through rain and illness to achieve their goal. The following day, Wednesday, the Galway

Independent did an article on us, and on Thursday we were the main feature in the Sports section of the Galway Advertiser. We thought we had enjoyed our press coverage by the time the Galway Tribune and the City Tribune featured us on Thursday and Friday respectively, until Sheila informed me that we got a mention in the Sunday People. Famous or what?

 The days that followed were terrific, with people congratulating both Francis and myself wherever we went. I was at the Millennium Park with the kids, when this guy came over and said, "Can I shake your hand?" He told me that he had met Richard Donovan, the multi-marathon runner, recently and now wanted to meet another world record holder. I was stoked. A few days later I met one of our physios, Maeve, while walking Spike. She said, "You're the tennis player aren't you? I attended your partner during the marathon." We had a chat and she thought that it was probably a record in itself that we didn't cramp during the 36 hours. I got lots of nice compliments as I walked the dog over the next few weeks, but the funniest incident happened when I met these two guys who, shall we say, had shared a few cans before I met them. Nicole was on her bike, and the dog was running ahead, when they stopped to talk. "You're the Tennis player, God! You're a mighty man, Mike." I thanked them for the compliment, and then they insisted on giving me a donation for the charities, providing I said a prayer for them. The only pity is that I didn't meet them before they fuelled up, as I might have collected more. However, when I recounted the events to Francis, he informed me that I was lucky, as they wouldn't have given him anything considering his brother had a dispute with one of them!

Francis and I had a target of between 3000 and 4000 in mind, and to bolster it we decided to run a table quiz. Diana Hogan Murphy, a friend and former mixed doubles partner of mine, had run a terrific event for Croi, and when I asked her would she help she took on the entire organisation of the event. It was a great success and, mainly due to Diana's hard work, we raised 800 in Massimo's, where a customer of my video library, Cian Campbell, kindly provided the location, finger food and the questions and answers, to ensure a great night and great boost to our fund. Cian asked me to be M.C. and I was in my element. Diana, Francis and I collected the answers and sold the raffle tickets and we were well supported with a great turnout, including Mark Griffin's family. We were still a little short of our target, so we organised a Bowling night, and this brought us up to 3600. Very fitting I thought, to match our 36 hours!

Whereas Francis and I both felt that we had done everything by the book, we still had to have the record verified by GWR. As Francis was in Dublin at the time, Marie and Sheila called out to my house on the Thursday after the event, and we went through the documentation. Both ladies were very thorough, and anything that needed to be added they promised to sort the next day. Marie noticed that one of the independent witnesses had used headed GLTC paper to write his letter, so I rang his wife and she kindly informed us that he would put it on his own paper and drop it into the club the next day. GWR are very particular about these things, so everything had to be spot on. Marie also noted that there could be no mention of us setting a new world record as GWR would have to verify it first, and fair play to Pat Diskin, a local journalist; he was first off the mark in The Examiner to state that we were awaiting verification from GWR for a new world record. " Subject to verification", is the nearest to an acknowledgement that you are allowed use before it is official. The three of us felt that we had done it right, and Marie, as in 2003, agreed to send off the details and confirm their arrival at Guinness World Records in London. Their website states that it could take six weeks to verify, and from then on Marie was checking the site. One night I logged on, having got the codes from Marie, and the site confirmed that it was processing our application. Marie rang, to be informed that there was a huge backlog as they get so many world record attempts per week. Marie and I kept in contact by text as we kept checking the net for further information. Finally on Monday

December 5th , I asked Michelle to check for news and got a terrific surprise. "Congratulations, Your record has been accepted as a new world record your certificates will follow shortly." As Edwin informed me when I contacted him, it was five months, to the date, that we started our record attempt. It was great to set the original record in 2003, but to create it, lose it and regain it, is far more satisfying. In November Francis and I were selected as Sport Stars of the Year for Tennis at the Galway Bay FM awards night, by Olly Turner, head of Sport at GBFM. I remember vividly when Olly and Jimmy Norman interviewed us prior to our first record attempt in 2003. On both occasions we were selected as sport stars of the week, but to take an award for tennis for the year really topped off our achievement.

Chapter 7

RECORD BREAKERS

How come the Irish, as a country, hold more world records per capita than any other? It's quite incredible when you think about it. One would assume the Americans, Japanese, Chinese or even the Russians, would far outnumber a small country of 4 million inhabitants when it comes to setting world records. Is it something in the Irish psyche, or mentality, that drives us to over-achieve? It's an interesting subject, and one which begs the question ...do we feel we have to prove ourselves constantly, and do we all believe that records are only made to be broken?

There is a common misconception in Sport, that the Irish are a nation who like to enjoy themselves, and, sure, if we win that's a bonus. We have a truly competitive nature, and speaking personally I have never bought in to the idea that it's the taking part that matters, not the winning. Take England, and a prime example would be Wimbledon. The last time, to date, an Englishman won the Championship, was 1936-with Fred Perry. When asked why, Perry expressed the view that until an English player was bloody-minded enough, this would not change. The Germans exude a teutonic approach, personified best by Boris Becker, when at 17 he powered his way to the Wimbledon title.

The Australians, I believe, have a terrific sporting record in recent years, and a great attitude. On the outside, they exude a real laid- back, good-humoured approach to life, where you would assume they are happiest downing a few tinnies, and enjoying a good Bar-B-Q. But behind the "sorry mate" apology from Pat Rafter, as he corrects his service toss-up, lies a fiercely competitive, highly motivated, fully confident, street fighter. They have a great mindset, in that they seem to be able to play hard and work hard. I believe that some nations, such as America and Britain, have superior attitudes to Sport, expecting to win. Whereas, the Australians and the Irish know that they have to be at their best to truly compete, at the highest levels. Both nations tend to produce athletes capable of living "in the now". At some point in your life, you find yourself in a position where you can accomplish something special, but not everyone can "grasp the nettle" and rise to the occasion.

To answer the question I posed earlier "What makes the Irish hold more world records than any other country?" you have to get inside the mindset of those that do it. Further on I will analyse the answers to a questionnaire on how this has occurred. Personally, I would say that it comes down to a number of factors: confidence, self-belief, dedication, preparation, an iron refusal to contemplate defeat or failure and.....luck. To attempt a world record you need supreme confidence. Think about it.... A world record... the best on the planet, on a given day. Don't think about it too much, or you will not do it. I have always believed that when you make a decision you go with it fully. There is no going back, or room for self-doubt. It doesn't matter if others doubt you, as long as you have self-belief. You must be dedicated to your cause. If you do not believe in it, then it is not worth doing, and you will not give it your best. To quote Roy Keane: "Fail to prepare, Prepare to fail." You must plan for every contingency. Nothing should prevent you from achieving your goal. You must never contemplate defeat. Once you are competing, you must give everything, and leave no regrets behind you. The last factor, the great imponderable...luck! Some say that you make your own luck, but you never know, and you know what they say about "the luck of the Irish."

Chapter 8

MOTIVATION

So what motivates people to set world records, or even to attempt to set/break a record? I have always been interested in Sport Psychology, and finding out what drives or motivates people to achieve/strive for excellence in their profession. We all have basic motives, and Maslow developed a Hierarchy of Needs. (A.H. Maslow: Motivation and Personality 1954) His theory was that the lower needs have to be at least partially satisfied, before the higher needs can become important sources of motivation. We begin with physiological needs, such as hunger, before moving up the scale to safety needs, (belongingness, esteem), cognitive needs (to understand), aesthetic needs such as order and beauty; to the highest needs of self-actualisation: the need to find self-fulfilment and to realize one's potential. These are the reasons that I believe some of us are motivated and driven to achieve our goals.

Motivation is not all about being 'psyched up' or positive thinking. To be properly motivated, I believe that you must have controllable and realistic objectives. For example, in our record attempt we set out to play for 26 hours, and were able to organise people to help us attain our goal. We set a realistic target, and set up a proper environment, where if everything went to plan our objective was attainable. There are different types of motivation. There is intrinsic motivation:-where an activity is performed for itself, and judgement is based on how the individual performs, or more accurately, the individual's perception of performance. Extrinsic motivation is viewed more as a means to an end. It deals with constraints such as opponents, and rewards such as money or trophies. Extrinsic motives are more ego oriented, and are concerned with defeating others. Intrinsic motives provide experiential rewards, and generally put the individual under less pressure, whereas extrinsic motives provide social or objective rewards, and put more pressure on the individual. A simple rationalisation of the two forms may conclude that intrinsic motivation is more concerned with performance, with extrinsic motivation more concerned with achievement, or the end result. Given that it comes down to the importance of experiencing the action and enjoying the participation, versus the achievement or end goal, I would conclude that those individuals who are mainly extrinsically motivated are more likely to set records than the intrinsically motivated individual, who derives satisfaction from achieving their own personal best.

Those individuals who are extrinsically motivated must balance the need for achievement with the fear of failure. That is why it is important to seek challenges, but set realistic objectives. Intrinsically motivated people tend to be task-oriented, where performance is paramount, whereas extrinsically motivated people tend to be more ego oriented, with their perception of success or failure relating to the attainments of others. The bottom line for these individuals is winning. To those more qualified to make judgement on this interpretation, this may seem a simplistic view of personality types, however I will attempt to explore it more in the interview section of this book. I consider myself to be extrinsically motivated, in my attitude to sport and life. I have always set my standards against others, and feel that it is important to compete with the intention to surpass others' achievements. On undertaking our record attempt, Francis and I set out to break the perceived record of 24 hours and 24 minutes, and neither of us would have been satisfied with less. As it turned out, we actually set a new record, which is an even more satisfying achievement, as nobody had attempted what we did previously. The 24 hour 24 minute record was in fact for singles, and the new record we set was for one pair taking on all-comers. If anything we were both even more motivated second time round! We were determined to reclaim our world record once we heard a German pair had surpassed our original achievement. We set out not just to break their record but also to extend it, and raise the bar for future generations.

There is a tremendous sense of achievement and accomplishment in attaining your goal, and in my opinion the drive to do this must come from within. Nobody can create the desire to achieve your goal unless you really want it yourself. The old expression of 'leading a horse to water but not being able to make the horse drink', is very relevant to achieving self-fulfilment and reaching one's potential. From the origin of the idea of setting a world record, to the completion of the journey and attainment of a personal goal, it has been a profoundly satisfying experience for me, and I am sure, all those who have entered the Guinness Book of Records and will forever be known as world record setters.

A can-do positive attitude is very important when setting goals. If you look at most successful people you will notice that many of them share common features. The mix often contains self-confidence, a positive outlook on life and an inner belief that if they try their best that they will succeed. I remember reading that Jimmy Connors once said that he hated losing more than he loved winning. That, for me, really sums up the concept of extrinsic motivation. Whereas intrinsic motivation would indicate that if an individual performed to their capabilities, or as well as they could, they would derive satisfaction from that, I feel that from Connors' attitude, performance itself was not enough; victory must be achieved for the individual to accomplish their goal, and then one can be satisfied. I suppose it comes down to attitudes to life, and whether one is willing to settle for second best. Viewing great sportsmen like Jimmy Connors or Roy Keane, you get the impression that winning isn't everything; it is the only thing. In both these individuals, you feel that they always give of their best, and feel that to do any less would be cheating themselves. It's often been said that to beat Connors, you would have to drive a stake through his heart! This is obviously due to the fact that Jimmy was well known for great fight-backs. I see a similar attitude in Serena Williams who, despite being injured in the Final of The Australian Open in 2005, in the first game against Lindsay Davenport, found a way to dig deep and went on to win. I believe that this performance had as much to do with mental strength or fortitude, as it had with the physical side of Serena's game. She performed similarly in the season ending play-offs final in 2004 against Maria Sharapova. Despite hardly being able to serve, she battled to a 4-0 lead in the final set, before her body let her down, and Sharapova, another mentally tough player, found a way to beat her.

Tennis is a sport where mental toughness plays a major part. John Newcombe claimed that the Australian coaching system embraced the science of Sport Psychology at a very early stage. Mike Tyson believed that next to boxing, tennis was the toughest one-on-one sport, as the two individuals pitted their wits against each other in battle. Some players like Ivan Lendl seemed to use their skills in another one-on-one sport, chess, to enable them to break down opponents and find a way to win. Bjorn Borg appeared to use incredible powers of concentration, as he blocked out distraction with incredible focus, on his way to back-to-back French and Wimbledon titles between 1976 and 1980. Various suggestions have been put forward over time, on what the ratio of mental strength to physical attributes is at the highest level of tennis. I believe that of 90:10 to be accurate, if you take that all players on the Men's Tour ranked in the top 100 would have basically the same techniques and physical attributes. Given that you have varying heights and weight statistics, and that all 100 players have a certain mastery of strokes and technique, the top few have a certain edge on the rest. That edge, in my belief, is psychological. I also believe, that the top performers in all sports have that edge on their fellow competitors. What does it comprise of? Could it be a stronger personal belief in accomplishing goals than the ordinary person, positive life attitude, the lack of fear in putting one's reputation on the line, the adrenaline rush to accomplish more than others and raise the bar? To paraphrase J.F.K. 'Some people, when faced with challenges in life, ask why; others say why not and accept the challenge.'

To conclude, in my opinion those people who are extrinsically motivated, are more likely to attempt setting records, than those whose intrinsic motivation is related to the performance of the task itself. To give oneself the optimum conditions, you need to set realistic and attainable goals. Never underestimate the role played by the mind, especially in endurance-related activity such as a world record. You cannot contemplate failure; your body should be physically prepared to endure the task. Positive imagery, allied with a positive support group, will see you break through the wall that most people hit before the end goal is clearly in sight. If you have absolute belief in yourself, this will transfer to all those around you, and together you will find that most goals are achievable.

Chapter 9

IRISH WORLD RECORD HOLDERS

In the autumn of 2005, while we awaited validation of our second world record, I decided to continue my research into the psyche of world record holders, by putting an advertisement in the national newspapers, to contact other Irish world record holders. As GWR had not being willing to provide me with a list of Irish record holders, and the 2005 Anniversary Edition only provided a limited number, I decided to try this avenue of contacting others. I advertised for a week in the Irish Independent and the Evening Herald, and was pleasantly surprised with the reaction. The first person I spoke to was Robert O' Farrell, who had trained the youngest dog in the world to win an open all-age championship qualifying field trial, at eight months and one day. He was delighted to discuss his achievement, a record that still stood after thirty three years. I sent a questionnaire to all those record holders, past and present, that I spoke with, and Robert's tallied extremely close to the components that I had felt applied to the kind of people who attempt world records. He appeared confident, dedicated, extremely well prepared, very motivated to achieve something that had not been done before, holding a solid refusal to contemplate defeat in his efforts, despite being fully aware that what appeared almost impossible was steeped in uncertainty (his own words), held a lot of self belief and elation at accomplishing his goal. Robert showed both intrinsic and extrinsic characteristics in his answers, however I believe that the extrinsic factors weighed heavier, as he was attempting to accomplish something which had not been done before, and this was his main motivation. It was wonderful to note that he viewed it as performing a feat of distinction, as it is important to remember that he did set a new world record!

Julia Galvin contacted me next, and she had set a world record for mountain bike bog snorkelling, in 2004. This sport, which is also very popular in Wales, is creating a lot of interest, and Julia has many contacts that have attempted world records in different feats in recent times. Whereas Robert was very goal-oriented, I felt that Julia really enjoyed the fun element as much as the challenge of attempting world records. I can certainly see this lady creating many world records if her enthusiasm is anything to go by. Of the many contacts that Julia gave me, I had very interesting conversations with Brendan Morrissey and Paul Roberts. Brendan had attempted to set a record for hand shaking at the National Ploughing Championships. He shook 14,169 hands in eight hours, and for his next task he was organising an event with the most Honda-50 motorbikes in one place, at the Culchee Festival in October 2005. I believe this record is currently awaiting verification. To quote my former teacher and independent witness at both tennis marathons, Brendan Kelly; "More power to you Brendan!" Paul Roberts, at the time I spoke to him, was the strongest man in Ireland; I wasn't going to argue the point with him! Paul had carried Julia in the World Wife Carrying Competition in Finland, and held many Irish records. I believe that it's only a matter of time before he adds world records to his C.V.

Richard Donovan is our local multi-marathon man in Galway, and you could fill a book with his achievements and insights alone, on the whole process of setting world records. I often meet Richard out training on the river walkway near my home, when I walk my dog. He responded to my questionnaire with a very interesting recollection of his three world records on a treadmill in the summer of 2003. Richard ran on a treadmill for over 27 hours in a 48 hour period, in Bar Cuba in Galway in July 2003, setting new world records for the 100k, 100 miles and 48 hours as recognised by GWR. These are only the tip of the iceberg when you consider the amount of records this uber-athlete has set in recent years, be it marathons in the South Pole, or across Ireland, he has done it all. I was very interested to read that even though he considered the GWR as part of the entertainment industry, he did feel that they were good guides, and that achievement depended very much on the quality of the record. I would have to agree wholeheartedly with Richard on this, and obviously feel that a lot more dedication and preparation go into running a marathon on ice and playing competitive tennis for 36 hours, than growing the longest nails or being the dog with the biggest ears! However I guess the total disparity in the type of records that exist is what makes the Guinness Book of World Records so unique, and of interest to so many people for different reasons. Vive le difference! It was obvious from reading his report that Richard prepares meticulously for every attempt, down to checking on the net (as we did) prior to his starting, so he knows exactly what has to be done.

At the 50th anniversary party for GWR in Dublin in 2004, I met Jim Payne, another multi-record setter, who had set a record for the most skips of a rope in 24 hours, of 141,221. He was telling me that he was contemplating using a skipping rope to complete the Dublin City Marathon. Considering the dedication that he has shown to date I don't doubt that he will succeed. There are so many Irish world records set, that it would take another book to compile them, and it is a great honour for Francis and myself to join this list of achievers. Just to mention some of those we featured alongside in the 50th edition, and give you some idea of the variety of records held by the determined Irish; there was Paddy Doyle, another multi-record setter who held the record for the greatest height attained on a climbing machine in one hour, Sonia O' Sullivan for the fastest 2000 metres race, Richard Donovan for the fastest 100km on a treadmill, Eamonn Keane for the most accumulative weight bench pressed in one hour, from the world of Entertainment (which, according to Richard Donovan, we can all claim to feature in) we were joined by West life and U2, as well as actors Peter O' Toole and Barry Fitzgerald, and the world record for the most people at a table quiz was set at the Radisson in Galway. To top it off, as a nation, we Irish boast the highest tea consumption per capita, at 1,184 cups per person per year. I will definitely drink to that! So if you think that you would like to add to this ever-growing list, then remember that to do so takes a lot of dedication, self-belief, a good support team, thorough preparation and a stout refusal to contemplate defeat. Good luck!

QUESTIONNAIRE

Dear,

        I am currently researching a book on Irish World Record Holders. As you are a member of this elite club I would be grateful if you could take the time to fill out this questionnaire in block capitals please and return it to me as soon as possible:

What record(s) did you set?

Why did you decide to attempt this record?

Give a brief summary of the organisation involved in setting up your attempt.

What was the most difficult aspect involved in your preparation?

What support team did you have and how important were they?

What was the most difficult part of the record attempt for you personally?

Did you hit 'the wall'?

Did you at any stage question why you attempted the record?

Did you at any stage think that you would not achieve your goal?

Was there in your opinion a general belief among your support team/those watching that you would be successful?

How did you feel once you had completed your attempt?

Was there any doubt that your record attempt would not be verified by GWR?

How important was it to you that your record be included in the Guinness Book of Records?

What does being a World Record Holder mean to you personally?

What characteristics do you believe that yourself and other world record holders have that motivated you to accomplish this particular goal?

What advice would you give to someone contemplating an attempt at a world record?

Thank you for participating I will keep you informed of any further progress as regards the book.

Yours in Sport & Health

Mike Geraghty, 5 Upper Newcastle, Galway. 091/525022.

24 UPPER NEWCASTLE
GALWAY
527452/525022
21/5/03.

DEAR

    I AM ORGANISING A TENNIS MARATHON STARTING AT 2 PM ON FRI JUNE 20TH.
THIS WILL BE AN ATTEMPT TO SET A RECORD FOR 2 PLAYERS TAKING ON ALL-COMERS IN THE
GUINNESS BOOK OF RECORDS. ALL MONEY RAISED AT THE EVENT WILL BE DONATED TO THE
CO GALWAY BRANCH OF THE MENTALLY-HANDICAPPED ASSOCIATION. THE GUINNESS RECORDS
ORGN ARE VERY STRICT ON EVERYTHING BEING DONE BY THE BOOK. TO QUALIFY AS A LEGITI-
MATE RECORD WE HAVE TO STICK RIGIDLY TO THEIR GUIDELINES. AS WELL AS KEEPING
RECORDS OF OPPONENTS, BREAKS, INDEPENDENT WITNESSES, STEWARDS, PHOTOGRAPHIC
AND VIDEO EVIDENCE WE NEED MEDICALLY QUALIFIED PEOPLE AVAILABLE THROUGHOUT THE
EVENT. SO TO MAKE THIS HAPPEN WE NEED DOCTORS/NURSES /ORDER OF MALTA QUALIFIED
PEOPLE ETC TO ENSURE THE PARTICIPANTS ARE SAFE. WHEREAS I APPRECIATE THAT IT WOULD
BE IMPRACTICAL TO HAVE A G.P./NURSE COURTSIDE IN 4 HOUR SHIFTS I AM TRYING TO PUT
TOGETHER A PANEL OF MEDICAL PEOPLE TO COVER THE EVENT. AT PRESENT THERE IS A
RECORD OF 24 HRS 20 MINS FOR SINGLES BUT, THERE IS NO OFFICIAL RECORD FOR DOUBLES.
THIS CAN ONLY BE DONE BY 2 PLAYERS TAKING ON ALL-COMERS ADHERING STRICTLY TO THE
RULES OF TENNIS. SO WE WILL PLAY SOME 3 SET AND SOME 5 SET MATCHES WITH THE USUAL
BREAKS TAKEN IN AN ACTUAL MATCH. THE TWO PLAYERS INVOLVED WILL BE FRANCIS POWER
AND MIKE GERAGHTY. IF WE CAN SET A RECORD AND WE NEED A LOT OF HELP TO DO SO WE
WILL BE RAISING MONEY FOR A GOOD CAUSE AND GETTING INVALUABLE PUBLICITY FOT
GLTC. WHAT WE NEED WOULD BE A COMMITMENT FROM MEDICAL PEOPLE TO BE AVAILABLE
TO COME IF NEEDED FOR A PARTICULAR TIME PERIOD. IF WE COULD CONTACT YOU BY
PHONE/IF YOU ARE NOT TOO FAR AWAY YOU COULD POP BY FOR A SPOT CHECK. THIS SHOULD
BE SUFFICIENT TO COVER US FOR RECORD PURPOSES AND HOPEFULLY WE WOULD NOT
NEED TO TROUBLE YOU EXCEPT TO SIGN A NOTE SAYING THAT YOU WERE AVAILABLE IF NEED-
ED. EVERY RECORD ATTEMPT NEEDS SOME MEDICAL ATTENTION AND WE WOULD BE VERY
GRATEFUL AT GLTC IF YOU COULD HELP US OUT.

THERE WILL BE A SHEET AVAILABLE AT RECEPTION (522353) TO
FILL IN TIME-SLOTS FROM 2 PM FRI 20/6 TO PROVISIONALLY 4PM SAT 21/6. ALTERNATIVELY YOU
CAN CALL ME AT THE PHONE NUMBERS ABOVE. I WOULD BE GRATEFUL FOR ANY ADVICE ON
PREPARATION FOR THE EVENT OR ON HOW BEST TO COPE DURING IT.

YOURS IN TENNIS,

MIKE GERAGHTY DIRECTOR GLTC
(Request for medical assistance for tennis marathon 2003).

TENNIS MARATHON

THERE WILL BE AN ATTEMPT TO SET A RECORD FOR A DOUBLES MARATHON ON FRIDAY JUNE 20TH 2003 AT GLTC STARTING AT 2PM AND HOPEFULLY RUNNING INTO SATURDAY JUNE 21ST. I HAVE ASKED THE TENNIS COMMITTEE FOR THE USE OF COURT 3 AS THERE WILL BE MATCHES IN THE CLUB CHAMPIONSHIPS FROM 7PM TO 10 PM FRI 20TH AND ON SAT 21ST AS WELL.

THERE IS AN EXISTING SINGLES RECORD OF 24 HRS AND 20 MINS BUT AT PRESENT THERE IS NO OFFICIAL RECORD FOR A DOUBLES TEAM TAKING ON ALL-COMERS. THE GUINNESS BOOK OF RECORDS WILL NOT RECOGNISE AS A RECORD A GROUP OF PLAYERS COMPETING OVER TIME. IT MUST BE THE SAME TWO AND THERE ARE VERY STRICT GUIDELINES TO QUALIFY TO BE RECOGNISED AS RECORD HOLDERS.

AUTHENTICATION:
1: SIGNED STATEMENTS BY 2 INDEPENDENT PERSONS OF SOME STANDING IN LOCAL COMMUNITY WHO HAVE ATTENDED THE EVENT AND CAN CONFIRM DETAILS OF THE CLAIM.
2: INDEPENENT CORROBORATION IN FORM OF MEDIA COVERAGE. AND A VHS VIDEO.
3: HIGH QUALITY COLOUR PHOTOGRAPHS.
4: A SIGNED AND DETAILED LOGBOOK SHOWING THAT THE EVENT HAS BEEN THE SUBJECT OF UNREMITTING SURVEILLANCE.

WE CANNOT USE GUINNESS WORLD RECORDS EXCEPT IN MIDDLE OF POSTER
I.E. TENNIS MARATHON ATTEMPT TO QUALIFY FOR GUINNESS BOOK OF RECORDS.

SAFETY:
CONTESTANTS NEED DOCTORS CERT TO COMPETE IN EVENT. NOBODY U-14 CAN COMPETE.
14-18 NEED PARENTAL PERMISSION (WRITTEN).
A FULLY QUALIFIED PRACTISING MEMBER OF MEDICAL PROFESSION MUST BE PRESENT AT ALL TIMES WATCHING THE EVENT. I`VE CHECKED WITH GUINNESS RECORDS PEOPLE AND AS LONG AS PERSON IS CLOSE BY I.E. DOCTORS/NURSES/ORDER OF MALTA/FIRST AIDERS, NEAR CLUB AND MAKING CHECKS WE SHOULD BE O.K. I DON`T SEE US GETTING TOO MANY DOC`S TO SIT COURTSIDE FOR 4 HR
SHIFTS.MARIE IS COMPILING A LIST OF DOC/NURSES FOR ME TO APPROACH.

OFFICIALS:
2 STEWARDS ON 4 HOURLY SHIFTS TO MAINTAIN LOG BOOK, REGISTER MEDICAL PERSONNEL OBTAIN SIGNATURES/ADDRESS OF WITNESSES. THE STEWARDS CAN ACT AS WITNESSES

WITNESSES CANNOT BE RELATED TO CONTESTANTS OR BE U-18.
THE MATCHES WILL BE VARIED IN LENGTH SOME 3 SET/5 SET. THE
ALL COMERS CAN BE EITHER MALE/FEMALE. PLAY WILL CONFORM
TO RULES OF TENNIS. THERE WILL HAVE TO BE A MASSIVE EFFORT
PUT IN BY CLUB MEMBERS TO MAKE THIS A SUCCESS. I PROPOSE
THAT GLTC DO THE MARATHON TO RAISE MONEY FOR THE MENTAL
LY HANDI-CAPPED AND THAT ANY MONEY TAKEN IN BE DONATED
TO THE CO. GALWAY BRANCH OF THIS ASSOCIATION. THE TWO
CONTESTANTS WILL HAVE CARDS FOR DONATIONS AND ALL THOSE
WHO PARTICIPATE IN THE ATTEMPTED RECORD WILL BE ASKED TO
MAKE A DONATION. I PROPOSE THAT THE BOARD GIVE THE COURT
FREE OF CHARGE WITH A DEDUCTION FOR FLOODLIGHTS. WE WILL
BE LOOKING FOR A LOT OF PLAYERS, WITNESSES/STEWARDS, 2
INDEPENDENT WITNESSES TO OVERSEE THE WHOLE EVENT,
PRESS/TV COVERAGE,VIDEO/PHOTO COVERAGE, SPONSORS FOR
TENNIS BALLS, FOOD, ETC. A LARGE CLOCK SHOULD BE VISIBLE,
LOTS OF ACTIVITIES TO KEEP THE CLUB LIVELY E.G. MUSIC/BAR-B-
Q/VIDEOS IN BAR/FACILITIES FOR PLAYERS/OFFICIALS ETC.
TO QUALIFY FOR THE GUINNESS BOOK OF RECORDS WE HAVE TO
DO IT BY THE BOOK.GLTC WILL GET GREAT PUBLICITY IF WE SET A
RECORD AND WE WILL ALSO BE MAKING A CONTRIBUTION TO A
WORTHWHILE ORGANISATION IN THE CO GALWAY BRANCH OF THE
MENTALLY HANDI-CAPPED. I HAVE A CLAIM NO SINCE LAST SEP
TEMBER AND HAVE BEEN IN CONTACT WITH THE GUINNESS WORLD
RECORD PEOPLE ON A FEW OCCASIONS.THE TWO PLAYERS WHO
WILL BE TAKING ON ALL COMERS ARE FRANCIS POWER AND MIKE
GERAGHTY. MAY THE FORCE BE WITH US.

MIKE GERAGHTY DIRECTOR GLTC
(Document on task ahead for information for the Board of Directors Gltc 2003).

(Postscript: There was some confusion with GWR in the build up to the world record attempt whether there was a doubles world record for 24 hrs, 24 mins or if this just related to singles. So Francis and Mike set this as the target to beat).

GALWAY DUO NET NEW WORLD RECORD

50 years ago on 6th May 1954, Roger Bannister broke the four minute mile barrier, with a time of 3 mins 59.4 secs, and announcer Norris McWhirter called it " a new world record". He and his brother, Ross, were then commissioned by Sir Hugh Beaver, managing director of Guinness Brewery, a man who liked the idea of a book of superlatives, to produce the inaugural Guinness Book of Records a year later on 27th August 1955. In 2003 the 100 millionth copy of the book was published, and today 3 1/2 million copies of Guinness World Records are sold annually, showing mankind's desire for knowledge, combined with a passion to be a world record holder, is undiminished.

Two tennis players from Newcastle, Mike Geraghty and Francis Power, joined the unique club of world record holders on 20-21 June 2003, creating a New World Record for the longest competitive doubles tennis match, by one pair playing against all comers, lasting 26 hours at Galway Lawn Tennis Club. The cut off point for new records was May in 2003, so even though their record has stood for 15 months to date, it debuts in the prestigious 50th Anniversary Edition of Guinness World Records 2005.

The two Galway men now feature alongside Andy Roddick, Martina Navratilova, Bjorn Borg and Goran Ivanisevic, among others, in the tennis section of the book. They are absolutely delighted, as at any given time there are 30,000 different records competing to feature in the annual production. It is said that 13 year olds are the target market when GWR decide on the interest and appeal of each record. So, given that statistic, Mike and Francis can expect that there will be many challenges to their record in the future. At a time when Roger Federer is taking the men's game to a new level, this record proves that anything is indeed possible.

(This was a local press release on our entry into the Guinness Book of World Records).

WORLD RECORD SET AT GLTC

Between the hours of 2pm on Friday June 20th and 4pm Sat June 21st 2003, two Galway men, Mike Geraghty and Francis Power, set a world record for the longest competitive doubles match, by one pair playing against all comers, lasting 26 hours, at Galway Lawn Tennis Club. They played 14 different partnerships throughout the event, and raised 1200 for the Galway Branch of the Mentally Handicapped, in the process. Mike had the idea of running a Tennis Marathon over a weekend to raise money for charity and set a world record, but Guinness World Records informed him that the record would only stand if the same player/players were involved the whole time. So he persuaded Francis to team up and play for 26 hours as a marathon is 26 miles and it turned out to be a new world record!

There was a lot of organising involved in the event, and a sub-committee involving Marie Gordon (club administrator), Gai and Sinead Barry, Nicky Nash and Oliver Martyn, combined with the lads to ensure everything ran smoothly. This involved getting independent witnesses, stewards, doctors, physios, publicity etc. The two P.RO.s, Oliver (tennis cttee) and Gai (board of mgt), achieved coverage in all the local press and Galway Bay FM as well as the Daily Mirror, Irish Star and Examiner. Paddy Power was taking odds of 3/1 against, but unfortunately the lads were not aware of this, and did not manage to put a wager on.

 People literally came out of the woodwork on the Saturday to see history taking place at Threadneedle Road. It was terrific for the two players from Newcastle to see family, friends, club members old and new and particularly Donal Dempsey, who symbolises all that is good at Galway Lawn Tennis Club, cheer them on as they reached their goal of setting a world record for the Tennis Marathon. Ralph O` Gorman commentating for Galway Bay Fm live from Thread needle Rd, summed it up best with the immortal words "on the day that Nelson Mandela visited Galway and The Special Olympics were taking place in Dublin two Galway men are setting a world record for tennis." The following year Mike and Francis entered the 5Oth anniversary edition of the Guinness World Records alongside other tennis world record holders such as Bjorn Borg, Andy Roddick and Martina Navratilova. Not a bad achievement for Galway Lawn Tennis Club!

(This was a brief summary for local historian Peadar O' Dowd for his History of Galway Lawn Tennis Club).

MATCH BY MATCH INDICES

NEW WORLD RECORD CREATED AT GALWAY LAWN TENNIS CLUB 20-21 JUNE 2003.

2-4pm	TommyHehir & Leah Smyth	6-3 3-6 7-6 0-3
4-6pm	Martin O Morain & Oliver Martyn	6-0 6-2 6-2 6-1
6-8pm	Angela Dowling & John Mangan	7-5 3-6 6-3 3-0
8-10pm	Tim Jones & Nicky Nash	4-6 7-5 6-4
10-12	Brian McGoldrick & John Fennelly	4-6 3-6
12-2am	Sinead Barry & Grainne Coll	6-4 6-3 6-3
2-4am	Matt O Connor & Micheal O' Morain	6-7 7-5
4-6 am	Margaret & Neil McLoughlin	6-4 1-6 1-6 0-2
6-8am	Terry Powell & Gai Barry	5-7 5-5
8-10am	Eimear O' Byrne & Denise Dunne	6-1 6-2 6-1
10-12	Marie Gordon & Sarah Caulfield	6-1 6-3 6-0
12-2pm	Francis O' Connell & Ronan Neacy	7-6 2-6
2-4pm	Pat Folan & Dabnet Heery	6-0 6-1 6-1
	Pat Folan & Olwyn Raftery	5-1

Matches : 14, Sets : 35+5 unfinished, 71% success rate, Games : 339, 59% won.
Witnesses to sign   for record verification purposes 93.

WORLD RECORD RECLAIMED AT GALWAY LAWN TENNIS CLUB 5-6 AUGUST 2005.

12-2pm	Frances & Helen Sheehan	6-0 6-0 6-2 6-2 6-4
2-4pm	Brian McGoldrick & Oliver Martyn	6-0 7-6 6-3
4-6pm	Gerard Brennan & Gavin Melody	6-2 6-0 6-3 6-0 1-1
6-8pm	Mark Smyth & Daniel Cluskey	2-6 2-6 2-6 2-2
8-10pm	Tomas Doorowski & Lubos Vqclavek	6-2 6-2 6-3
10-12	Nicky Nash & Magz Wilson	7-5 6-0 3-4
12-2am	Emer Hardiman & Sinead Barry	6-1 6-1 5-6
2-6am	Ciaran Gilchrist & Carl Falsey	6-4 2-6 5-7 1-6 5-4
6-8am	Gerard Flaherty & Edwin Brennan	6-3
	Neil McLoughlin & Emer Hardiman	1-6 0-2
8-10am	Diana Hogan-Murphy & Thereze Waldron	4-6 6-4 3-0
10-12	Ollie Raftery & Geoffrey Power	6-1 6-1 6-4
12-2pm	Donal Hegarty & Barry O' Donovan	3-6 0-6 5-3
2-4pm	Rita Halloran & Collette Murphy	6-4 6-3 4-1
4-6pm	Felim Cluskey & Dympna Ormond	7-5 6-4 2-2
6-8pm	Sinead & Gai Barry	6-0 6-0 6-1 6-0
8-10pm	Pat Folan & Ladislav Visizevslag	6-0 6-1 6-0 0-1
10-12	Tommy Hehir & Nicky Nash	6-3 3-6 6-2.

Matches : 18, Sets : 50+12 unfinished, 76% success rate, Games : 457, Won 62%.
Witnesses to sign for record verification purposes 483.